The Riddle of the Exporter

International Launch Plan ™

An 8 step process to conquer the world of exporting

e.e. eriksson

2012 © Taranis, LLC

International Launch Plan

Congratulations!

If you are reading this workbook, you have already recognized the importance of global trade to the future of your business. Exporting is complex but not impossible. Best of all, exporting when done correctly can be very profitable.

The Riddle of the Exporter International Launch Plan™ is a practical guide to exporting. Having spent 20 years in manufacturing, I wrote this workbook from the point of view of an entrepreneur rather than the government point of view. When finished, you will have the basics for an international business plan, giving you a roadmap for your product's first venture into exporting.

The International Launch Plan™ presents a repeatable eight-step process. It is intended to be used in conjunction with the 2-day training or optional DVD. Although, it must be taught sequentially, nothing about exporting follows a set order. For instance in order to determine your Landed Costs (Step #3: Market Entry) you must engage the services of a freight forwarder (Step #6: Transportation). For this reason it is best to go through the entire eight steps before you begin the worksheets for each step.

Exporting is exciting for many reasons; it can be profitable, creates jobs and contributes to a vibrant U.S. economy. It's time to "Get Excited About Exporting!"™

Elyse Eriksson
The Riddle of the Exporter
© 2012 Taranis, LLC

International Launch Plan

The Riddle of the Exporter International Launch Plan™
First Edition
Copyright© 2012 by Elyse Eriksson

Published by Taranis, LLC

All rights reserved. This book or DVD may not be used or reproduced in any manner, in whole or in part, stored in a retrieval system or transmitted in any form (electronic, mechanical, photocopied, recorded or other means) without written permission from the author, except as permitted by the United States copyright law.

No liability is assumed with respect to the use of information contained herein. While every precaution has been taken in the preparation of this book, the author assumes no responsibility for errors, omissions or changes in governing regulations that frequently occur. Neither is any liability assumed for damages resulting from the use of information contained herein.

Editing and layout by Copper Leaf Communications: www.copperleafcommunications.com

ISBN-13: 978-0-9882468-0-5

ISBN-10: 0988246805

Printed in the United States of America

For more information about The Riddle of the Exporter™ Training visit us at
www.riddleoftheexporter.com or contact Elyse Eriksson at elyseeriksson@gmail.com

International Launch Plan

- Step #1: Getting Started
- Step #2: Market Research
- Step #3: Market Entry
- Step #4: Legal
- Step #5: Regulatory Compliance
- Step #6: Transportation
- Step #7: Payments/Finance
- Step #8: Cultural

International Launch Plan

Table of Contents

- Glossary of Acronyms and Terms 8
- **Step #1: Getting Started** 9
  - 5 Ws of Getting Started 9
  - Step #1 Basics 10
  - What You Need To Do Checklist 11
  - Getting Started Notes 11
  - Additional Forms 12
    - Export Readiness Test 12
    - Export Readiness Assessment 12
    - SWOT International Product or Service Assessment 13
    - Initial Investment Costs 14
    - Management Team 14
    - How Will You Export? 14
- **Step #2: Market Research** 15
  - 5 Ws of Market Research 15
  - Step #2 Basics 16
  - What You Need To Do Checklist 17
  - Market Research Notes 17
  - Additional Forms 18
    - Do You Need a License to Export? 18
    - Requirements to Import to Country of Destination 18
    - Intentional Exporter Country Research 19
    - Country Ranking Scorecard 20
    - Qualitative Research/Considerations 20
    - Selection Criteria for Potential Overseas Partners 20
- **Step #3: Market Entry** 21
  - 5 Ws of Market Entry 21
  - Step #3 Basics 22
  - What You Need To Do Checklist 23
  - Market Entry Notes 23
  - Additional Forms 24
    - Top Three Ways to Attract Clients 24
    - Screening Services 24
    - List Ways Marketing Material Must Be Adapted for International Markets 24
    - Update Your Website for International Clients 24
    - Estimate Foreign Market Landed Cost 25
    - Additional Costs to Consider for Each Job 26
    - Pricing 27
- **Step #4: Legal** 28
  - 5 Ws of Legal 28
  - Step #4 Basics 29
  - What You Need To Do Checklist 30
  - Legal Notes 30
  - Additional Forms 31
    - Type of Representative/Partner That is Best for Your Company 31
    - Introductory Visit with ELAN and/or Contract Lawyer 31
    - Contract Check List Considerations 32
    - Level of IP Protection 33
    - Type of IP Protection Required 33
    - Intellectual Property Lawyer Initial Meeting 33
    - IP Plan 33
- **Step #5: Regulatory Compliance** 34
  - 5 Ws of Regulatory Compliance 34

International Launch Plan

Step #5 Basics 35
What You Need to Do Checklist 36
Regulatory Compliance Notes 36
Additional Forms 37
    Type of Export 37
    4 Questions to Determine if You Need a License 37
    7 Steps to Complete License Requirements 37
    Do you need a license? 40
    Export Compliance Manual 41
    Regulatory Compliance on the Other Side of the Ocean 41

Step #6: Transportation 42
5 Ws of Transportation 42
Step #6 Basics 43
What You Need to Do Checklist 44
Transportation Notes 44
Additional Forms 45
    Questionnaire for Choosing a Freight Forwarder 45
    Transportation Analysis 46
    Packaging and Unique Transportation Issues 46
    Small Shipments 47
    INCOTERMS® 48
    Documents 49
    Insurance 49

Step #7: Payments/Finance 50
5 Ws of Payments/Finance 50
Step #7 Basics 51
What You Need to Do Checklist 52
Payments/Finance Notes 52
Additional Forms 53
    Interview Questions for Your Bank 53
    Country Risk and Political Risk 53
    Country Specific Policies on Payment Procedures 54
    Individual Company Risk 54
    FX Risk 55
    Payment Risk Options 56
    Do You Qualify as an IC-DISC? 56
    Export Development and Working Capital 57
    Facilities Development Financing 57
    Financing for your International Buyers 57
    Risk Analysis Flow Chart 58

Step #8: Cultural 59
5 Ws of Cultural 59
Step #8 Basics 60
What You Need to Do Checklist 61
Cultural Notes 61
Additional Forms 62
    Country Cultural Research 62
    Business Cards 62
    Proper Protocol or Custom for Business Meetings 63
    Proper Protocol or Custom for Social Entertaining 63
    Taboos and Deal Breakers 64
    Negotiations 64

Appendix A: INCOTERMS® 65
Appendix B: Government Agencies and Other Regulations 66

International Launch Plan

Contact Information for Government Agencies Involved in the Export Process and Locations in the CFR (Code of Federal Regulations) 67
Appendix C: Sample Documents **69**
  Sales Representation and Distributorship Contract 69
  Pro Forma Invoice 71
  Commercial Invoice 72
  Bill of Lading 73
  Certificate of Origin 74
  Certificate of Insurance 75
  Key for 700 Format Specifications (Letter of Credit) 76
  Sample Letter of Credit Received Through SWIFT 77
  Export Compliance Manual 78

International Launch Plan

Glossary of Acronyms and Terms

3PL – Third Party Logistics	ICP - International Company Profile
AES - Automated Export System	IP - Intellectual Property
B/L – Bill of Lading	IPS - International Partner Search
BIS – Bureau of Industry and Security	ISPM-15 (pallet or crate seal for wood shipments)
BNA - Bureau of National Affairs	ITA – International Trade Administration
BOM – Bill of Material	ITAR – International Traffic in Arms Regulations
CCC - China Compulsory Certification	ITN - Internal Transaction Number
CCC - Commerce Country Chart	LC – Letter of Credit
CCG - Country Commercial Guide	LCL - Less than Container Load
CCL – Commerce Control List	MRA - Mutually Recognized Agreement
CE - Conformité Européenne	NAFTA - North American Free Trade Agreement
COO – Certificate of Origin	NAICS - North American Industry Classification System
DDTC - Directorate of Defense Trade Controls	NEI - National Export Initiative
DOC – Department of Commerce	NLR - No License Required
EAA – Export Administration Act	OEE - Office of Export Enforcement
EAR - Export Administration Regulations	OFAC - Office of Foreign Asset Control
ECCN - Export Control Classification Number	PCT - Patent Cooperation Treaty
EDA - Economic Development Alliance	POA - Power of Attorney
EEI - Electronic Export Information	REACH - Registration, Evaluation, Authorization of Chemicals
ELAN – Export Legal Assistance Network	RoHS - Restriction of Hazardous Substances
EMC – Export Management Company	SBDC - Small Business Development Center
EPA - Environment Protection Agency	Schedule B
ETC – Export Trading Company	SDN - Specially Designated Nationals
EWCP - Export Working Capital Program	SED – Shipper's Export Declaration
EXIM Bank – Export-Import Bank of the U.S.	SGS - Société Générale de Surveillance
FAS - Foreign Agricultural Services	SVHC - Substance of Very High Concern
FCC - Federal Communications Commission	SWIFT - Society for Worldwide Interbank Financial Telecommunications
FCL - Full Container Load	SWPM - Solid Wood Packaging Material
FCPA – Foreign Corrupt Practices Act	ULD - Unit Loading Device
FITA - Federation of International Trade Associations	USEAC – U.S. Export Assistance Center = U.S. Commercial Services = export.gov
FTA – Free Trade Agreement	USITC - U.S. International Trade Commission
FTZ – Foreign Trade Zone	USPPI - U.S. Principal Party of Interest
FX - Foreign Exchange	USTDA – U.S. Trade and Development Agency
GATT – General Agreement on Tariffs and Trade	USTR - U.S. Trade Representative
General Averaging - Maritime Law	WEEE - Waste of Electrical and Electronic Equipment
Gold Key Service	WIPO – World Intellectual Property Organization
HTS – Harmonized Tariff Schedule (#)	WTC - World Trade Center
ICE – U.S. Immigration and Customs Enforcement	

International Launch Plan Step #1

Step #1: Getting Started

5 Ws of Getting Started

Why is this step important?
To determine if exporting is a wise and profitable decision for your company?
If yes, determine the best method to export.

What do you need to know?  **What** do you need to do?
(see checklist)

- The key elements of export readiness to see if your company is a good fit
- Product assessment to determine if your product is marketable in foreign markets
- Personal and management commitment and assignment of duties
- Financial assessment to determine the financial commitments required
- How you want to export: directly or indirectly? Establish criteria for selection
- The government agencies that play a role in exporting.
- Do not forget that "Export Here = Import There"

Where do you go to find this information?
- www.export.gov
- www.fas.usda.gov (Foreign Agricultural Services)
- www.cia.gov/library
- www.export-u.com (free videos)
- www.globaledge.msu.edu (videos and country indices)
- www.i-b-t.net (sign up for email Q & A)
- www.ebsi.ie/ (fee based training, EU)
- www.sba.gov/content/small-business-development-centers-sbdcs/

Who can help you?
- 1-800-USA-TRAD(e) _____
- USEAC _____
- SBDC _____
- WTC or local economic development alliance _____
- Free Trade Alliance, San Antonio _____

When should you perform tasks?

- ▸ Export Readines Assessment
- ▸ Product Assessment
- ▸ Financial Assessment
- ▸ How do you want to export?

- ▸ Set up export team
- ▸ Search for distributor: EMC or ETC
- ▸ _____
- ▸ _____
- ▸ _____

Sidebar: DOC-Department of Commerce, EDA-Economic Development Alliance, EMC-Export Management Company, ETC-Export Trading Company, FAS- Foreign Agricultural Services, HTS- Harmonized Tariff Schedule (#) INCOTERMS, NAICS-North American Industry Classification System, NEI-National Export Initiative, SBDC-Small Business Development Center, Schedule B, USEAC-U.S. Export Assistance Center=DOC=U.S. Commercial Services = export.gov, WTC-World Trade Center

2012 © Taranis, LLC

International Launch Plan Step #1

Step #1 Basics

Benefits of Exporting

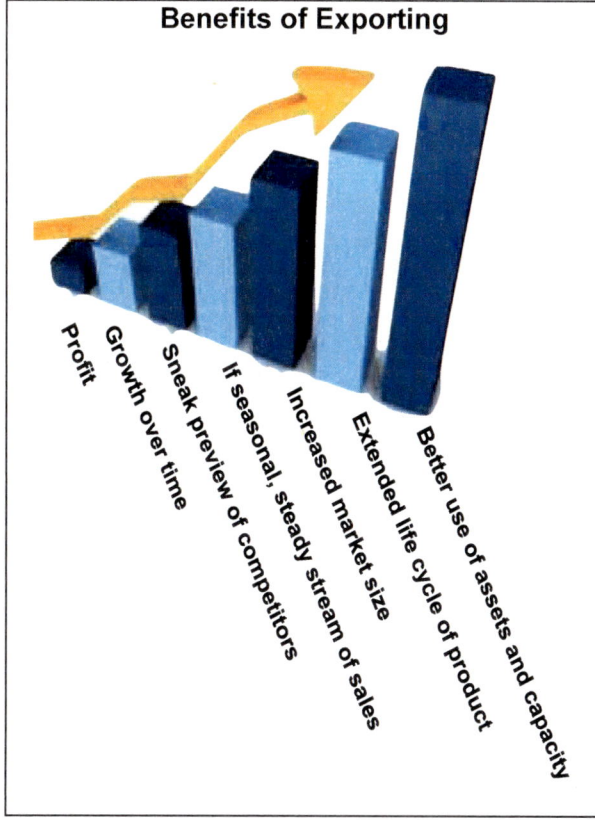

- Profit
- Growth over time
- Sneak preview of competitors
- If seasonal, steady stream of sales
- Increased market size
- Extended life cycle of product
- Better use of assets and capacity

2 Types of Exporters

Accidental — Request comes to you

Intentional — You decide

2 Methods of Exporting

Direct
In house export department, find your own distributors, sales reps

Indirect
Export Management Company (EMC), Export Trading Company (ETC)

Necessary Elements to be Successful in Exporting

- Viable, valuable product
- Can be adapted to foreign specifications and markets
- Capability to meet increased demand
- Management commitment
- Financial commitment
- Willingness to learn and an open mind
- Patience
- Adventurous spirit

Government Agencies Involved in Exporting (see Appendix C for a complete list)

 U.S. State Department-Directorate of Defense Trade Controls (DDTC)-defense articles & services, ITAR

 Commerce Department-Bureau of Industry and Security (BIS)-"dual use" items, EAR

 Treasury Department-Office of Foreign Assets Control (OFAC) oversees embargo and sanction lists

 Department of Homeland Security- Customs and Border Protection (CBP) enforces all exports at U.S. borders.

 Bureau of Census-trade-statistics and the AES

International LAUNCH Plan Step #1

What You Need To Do Checklist

- [ ] Take Export Readiness Test, see pg. 12
- [ ] Complete Export Readiness Assessment, see pg. 12
- [ ] Complete SWOT Product or Service Assessment, see pg. 13
- [ ] Create table to identify possible start up costs, see pg. 14
- [ ] Create management team listing, see pg. 14
- [ ] Decide how you will export, see pg. 14
- [ ] Cultural Communication affects every step of the eight-step process. What cultural issues should you consider with this step? (see Step #8)

Getting Started Notes

International Launch Plan Step #1

Additional Forms

Export Readiness Test

Questions	Low 1-3	Med 4-6	High 7-10
1. Are you prepared to devote additional time, effort and resources that will be required to become a successful exporter? If you are not the owner or the manager of the business, will the directors fully support you and recognize exporting as a legitimate activity and integral part of the company business plan?			
2. Are you able to identify unique features and qualities of your product and services that will enable you to exploit overseas market opportunities?			
3. Do you have sufficient financial strength and resources to develop overseas markets?			
4. Do you have the key players in your management team identified?			
5. Do you know if you want to export directly or indirectly?			
6. Does your business have a proven track record?			
7. Have you been contacted by international customers interested in your product? (Accidental Exporter)			
8. Are you interested in developing and expanding instead of servicing export markets? (Intentional Exporter)			
9. Can your products or services be modified to accommodate overseas market requirements if necessary?			
10. Have you researched the requirements to import into the country of interest?			
11. Do you have high quality promotional and marketing material?			
12. Do you have sufficient management skills and expertise to develop and service export markets? If not, could these be acquired?			
13. Do you have surplus capacity or the flexibility to expand production quickly if export orders are obtained?			
14. Do you have the willingness to pursue markets over a length of time?			
Total			

Export Readiness Assessment

Overall Score:	
Strong points:	
Weak points:	
Are there any deal breakers?	
Capability to correct weak points?	

2012 © Taranis, LLC

International Launch Plan Step #1

SWOT International Product or Service Assessment

Does your product have universal appeal or is its appeal country specific? If you offer services, what products can you use to piggyback? Each SWOT analysis will be a little different depending on the industry and product or process.

Product or Service Description _____
_____
_____
_____
_____

Strengths	Weaknesses
Opportunities	**Threats**

International Launch Plan Step #1

Initial Investment Costs
See Step #3: Market Entry, Additional Costs to Consider for Each Job.

Description	Cost
☐ Website updates to include translations, conversion links	
☐ Promotional materials	
☐ Additional personnel time for export market development	
☐ Product modifications	
☐ Label modifications	
☐ Market Research (free or fee based sites)	
☐ Training	
☐ Consultants	
☐ Legal	
☐ Travel	
☐ Trade shows	
☐ License fees if applicable	
☐ Testing fees if applicable	

Management Team

Job Title	Name
☐ Management Lead	
☐ Research Manager	
☐ Sales Manager	
☐ Logistics Manager	
☐ Compliance Manager	
☐ Accounting Manager	

How Will You Export?

Direct Export		Indirect Export (EMC/ETC)	
Pros	Cons	Pros	Cons
Options		Options	

Note: You may also want to consider franchising or licensing.

2012 © Taranis, LLC

International Launch Plan Step #2

Step #2: Market Research

5 Ws of Market Research

Why is this step important?

Any exporter, Accidental or Intentional has to know the legal requirements to export products from the US and import products into a foreign country.
If you plan to move from an Accidental Exporter to an Intentional Exporter, you will research, analyze and determine your best markets.

What do you need to know?  **What** do you need to do?
(see checklist)

- Mandatory research for Accidental and Intentional Exporters
- Become familiar with research tools (free and fee based) to provide initial and ongoing research to determine:
  1. Your product's NAICS and Schedule B numbers
  2. Product requirements to export from the US
  3. Product requirements to import into a foreign market
- Create a Country Ranking Scorecard to determine your market strategy

- 🚩 You cannot overestimate the importance of market research

Where do you go to find this information?
- www.export.gov   • www.fas.usda.gov   • www.naics.com
- tse.export.gov   • http://www.census.gov/foreign-trade/schedules/b/
- www.bis.doc.gov/licensing/exportingbasics.htm
- www.bna.com   • www.usatradeonline.gov   • www.referenceusagov.com
- data.worldbank.org/country
- www.kpmg.com/Global/en/WhoWeAre/Locations/Pages/Default.aspx
- Website for Customs or import government agency for destination country
- www.sba.gov/content/small-business-development-centers-sbdcs/
- www.globaltrade.net   • www.sbdcglobal.com
- www.ams.usda.gov/AMSv1.0/agtransportation
- Website for Customs

Who can help you?
- 1-800-USA-TRAD(e)
- U.S. Census /Commodity Analysis Branch 800-549-0595
- USEAC _____
- Foreign US Commercial Services, Chamber or Consulate _____
- SBDC _____
- WTC or local economic development alliance _____
- KPMG office in country _____
- Freight Forwarder _____

When should you perform tasks?

- ▸ Determine export requirements
- ▸ Determine destination import requirements
- ▸ Intentional Exporter research
- ▸ Country Ranking Scorecard

▸ Market Entry Plan of Action
▸ _____
▸ _____
▸ _____

Sidebar: BIS-Bureau of Industry & Security, BNA-Bureau of National Affairs, CCG- Country Commercial Guide, ECCN-Export Control Classification Number, FITA-Federation of International Trade Associations, FTA-Free Trade Agreement, INCOTERMS =FOB- Free on Board, IPS-International Partner Search, ITA-International Trade Administration, USEAC-U.S. Export Assistance Center=DOC=US Commercial Services = export.gov

2012 © Taranis, LLC

International Launch Plan Step #2

Step #2 Basics

Market Research is Essential
- What do you need to do to get your product out of the U.S.?
- What do you need to do to get it into another country?
- How do you plan to expand?

Example
Accidental Exporter: A client in Australia wants your product!
- What do you need to know to get your product out of the U.S. and into Australia?

Intentional Exporter: You decide to explore exporting to Japan and South Korea also
- Fill in the Country Ranking Scorecard to determine the best market

Country Ranking Scorecard

Country	Population	%	Rank	GDP per capita	%	Rank	Ease of doing business	%	Rank	Price	%	Rank	%	Rank	%	Rank	Final Rank
Australia																	
Japan																	
South Korea																	

The Most Important Numbers in Exporting
- NAICS - North American Industry Classification System
- Schedule B - the export version of a Harmonized Tariff Schedule Number found at census.gov

FTAs (Free Trade Agreements)...
Are like women: can't live with em can't live without em!
- Why we can't live without em? Without FTAs, U.S. exporters must add in much higher duties into their Landed Costs thus making the selling price for their goods non competitive.
- Why we can't live with em? FTA documentation is time consuming and carries civil and criminal penalties for false information. ** You are never required to claim FTA status.

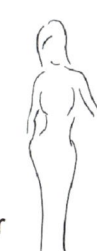

2012 © Taranis, LLC

International Launch Plan Step #2

What You Need To Do Checklist

- [ ] Find your NAICS#, see pg. 18
- [ ] Find your Schedule B#, see pg. 18
- [ ] Do you need a license to export from the U.S.?, see pg. 18 (see Step #5: Compliance)
- [ ] Determine requirements to import to country of destination, see pg. 18
- [ ] Research potential countries of destination and expansion for Intentional Exporters, see pg. 19
- [ ] Create Country Ranking Scorecard, see pg. 20
- [ ] List selection criteria for potential overseas partners, see pg. 20
- [ ] Cultural Communication affects every step of the eight-step process. What cultural issues should you consider with this step? (see Step #8)

Market Research Notes

International Launch Plan Step #2

Additional Forms
- [ ] Find your NAICS#_____ (see http://www.naics.com)
- [ ] Find your Schedule B#_____
  (see http://www.census.gov/foreign-trade/schedules/b/)
  Note: Technical products may require engineering assistance or assistance from U.S. Census Commodity Branch (1-800-549-0595).

Do You Need a License to Export?
If you answer YES to any one of these questions, you may need a license.
(see Step #5: Compliance and http://www.bis.doc.gov/licensing/exportingbasics.htm)

Ws	Question	Answer
What	1. Is my product a "dual use" item? Is it a commercial item that has potential for military use?	
Who	2. Is the person receiving my item a prohibited recipient?	
Where	3. Is the country of destination a prohibited country of shipment?	
How	4. Could the end use of my product be threatening to the United States or its citizens?	

Requirements to Import to Country of Destination
Country Name: _____

See www.export.gov, 1-800 USA-TRAD(e) and www.bna.com

Description	Requirement
[ ] Country Import Tariffs	
[ ] Labeling requirements	
[ ] Legal entity requirements	
[ ] Product specific requirements per country (e.g. food, health products)	
[ ]	
[ ]	

2012 © Taranis, LLC

International Launch Plan Step #2

Intentional Exporter Country Research

Country Commercial Guide (important chapters)
- ☐ Chapter 1: Overview
- ☐ Chapter 3: Selling U.S. Products & Services
- ☐ Chapter 5: Trade Regulations, Customs and Standards
- ☐ Chapter 9: Contact, Market Research and Trade Events

Country Indicators for _____ (see www.globaledge.msu.edu)
- ☐ Ease of Doing Business Rank # _____ of _____
- ☐ Global Connectedness Index Rank # _____ of _____
- ☐ Global Competitive Report Rank # _____ of _____
- ☐ Global Enabling Trade Report Rank # _____ of _____
- ☐ Global Manufacturing Competitiveness Index Rank # _____ of _____
- ☐ Global Services Location Index (outsourcing) Rank # _____ of _____
- ☐ Economic Freedom Index Rank # _____ of _____
- ☐ Tax Misery and Reform Report Rank # _____ of _____
- ☐ KOF Index of Globalization Rank # _____ of _____

First Questions to Answer for a Successful Market Entry Plan

Question	Answer
What are the characteristics of your perfect customer?	
How will your customer find you, your product or service?	
How will you get your product or service to this customer?	
Who will you need to help you get your product or service to the customer? (Some possibilities include a sales rep, distributor, individual store, EMC/ETC)	
What other products or services already exist that are similar to yours?	

2012 © Taranis, LLC

International Launch Plan Step #2

Country Ranking Scorecard

To complete the Country Ranking Scorecard:
1. Choose three potential countries to research
2. Set your criteria to determine their ranking
3. Conduct research
4. Rank
5. Combine with qualitative considerations

Country	Population	%	Rank	GDP per capita	%	Rank	Ease of doing business	%	Rank	Price	%	Rank		%	Rank		%	Rank	Final Rank

Qualitative Research/Considerations

_____
_____
_____
_____

Hint: Attend a local international chamber (like the French-American Chamber of Commerce) and conduct your own informal qualitative research. See Step #4: Legal for contract checklist considerations.

Selection Criteria for Potential Overseas Partners

Considerations	Answer
☐ Do you want a sole-proprietor or multi-company partner?	
☐ Years in business	
☐ Good credit	
☐ Expertise	
☐ Current market share	
☐ Exclusivity	
☐ Are you one of 5 or 500 companies they represent?	
☐ Territory	
☐ Title of goods	
☐ Payment terms on goods from overseas partner to you	
☐ Payment terms on commission to overseas partner	
☐ Non-performance clause	
☐ Warranty and returns	
☐	
☐	

2012 © Taranis, LLC

International Launch Plan Step #3

Step #3: Market Entry

5 Ws of Market Entry

Why is this step important?

Once you have determined where you want to be (perfect customer, market of entry and best channel of distribution) you must figure out how to reach your market. Before proceeding, every partnership (no exceptions) should undergo a thorough credit check (see Step #7).
You will need to estimate your product pricing, including all Landed Costs, to make sure you can be competitive.

What do you need to know?  **What** do you need to do?
(see checklist)

- Finalize the results of your Country Ranking Scorecard (quantitative) with the desired criteria you want in a potential overseas partner (qualitative) to determine your market entry strategy
- Determine your optimum pricing that compliments your market entry strategy
- Discover options for marketing your product to overseas partners/customers
- Update marketing materials for an international audience
- Analyze your website to update for international buyers
- Utilize the many government services to find and qualify partner/customers
- Estimate your true Landed Costs so that your pricing is competitive
- Do not forget there is no good substitute for a FACE-TO-FACE meeting

Where do you go to find this information?
- www.export.gov • www.thinkglobal.us/ • www.globaltrade.net
- www.fita.org/conferences.html • www.reedexpo.com/
- www.sbdcglobal.com • www.exportpro.com (Leif Holmvall)
- www.tradeshowalerts.com/merchant-exporters/index.html
- www.sba.gov/content/small-business-development-centers-sbdcs/

Who can help you?
- 1-800-USA-TRAD(e) _____
- USEAC _____
- SBDC _____
- WTC or local economic development alliance _____
- Foreign US Commercial Services Office _____
- Foreign Chamber of Commerce _____
- Trade Show Exhibit Staff or Salesman _____
- International Chambers of Commerce in your area for qualitative research

When should you perform tasks?

- ▸ Finalize market entry strategy
- ▸ Review marketing material
- ▸ Determine method of advertising
- ▸ Begin trade fair search (6-9 months out)

- ▸ Create Prospectus
- ▸ Update website
- ▸ Research IP protection <u>before</u> attending trade shows
- ▸ _____

FITA-Federation of International Trade Associations, GOLD KEY, INCOTERMS = CIF Cost Insurance and Freight, FOB-Free On Board, IPS-International Partner Search, OFAC-Office of Foreign Asset Control, USEAC-U.S. Export Assistance Center = U.S. Commercial Services = DOC = www.export.gov

2012 © Taranis, LLC

International LAUNCH Plan Step #3

Step #3 Basics

Market Questions: Are you selling apples or oranges?
- Who is your perfect customer?
- Where is your best country of export?
- Therefore who is your perfect customer in the best country of export?
- Does your client want apples or oranges?
- Apples in Japan or Australia?
- How do you find the perfect customer that wants to buy your apple products in Japan?

Pricing

- What is your Landed Cost? (The complete cost to take your product from here to there, including all sorts of hidden costs that you are going to uncover!)
- What is the optimum price to sell to your customer (subtracting the share of the profit taken by the distributor(s) in between)?
- Any profit left for you?

Marketing Plan
- Create your prospectus and a marketing plan
- Use all of the USEACs opportunities to reach out to new customers/partners
- USEAC = U.S. Export Assistance Center = U.S. Commercial Services = export.gov = 1-800-USA-TRAD(e)

Note: When deciding on a distributor, do not take the first offer. This is like a job interview. Find the best match for both sides.

2012 © Taranis, LLC

International Launch Plan Step #3

What You Need To Do Checklist

- [ ] List top three ways that you will attract clients with pros/cons of each (e.g. trade show, US Commercial News, Gold Key), see pg. 24
- [ ] List screening services, see pg. 24
- [ ] List ways that your marketing material must be adapted for your international market, see pg. 24
- [ ] Update your website for international clients, see pg. 24
- [ ] Estimate foreign market Landed Cost, see pg. 25-26
- [ ] Explore pricing options, see pg. 27
- [ ] Cultural Communication affects every step of the eight-step process. What cultural issues should you consider with this step? (see Step #8)

Market Entry Notes

International Launch Plan Step #3

Additional Forms

Top Three Ways to Attract Clients

Note: This will help you define your market so you know where to look.

Description	Target Audience	Cost	Pros	Cons

Screening Services

Note: This will help you find the right partner and eliminate prohibited partners.

Description	Cost	Partners' Rating	Comments
Gold Key			
IPS (International Partner Search)			
D & B			
Local country credit reports			
BIS (Bureau of Industry and Security)			

List Ways Marketing Material Must Be Adapted for International Markets

_____
_____
_____
_____
_____

Update Your Website for International Clients

- [ ] Translations
- [ ] International tab and contact person in company that handles international orders
- [ ] Size charts, conversions and comparisons, weight/dimension conversion link
- [ ] Contract or agreement addressing warranty, returns, Export Administrations Regulations and License Requirements if applicable
- [ ] Shipping estimate including import duties and insurance
- [ ] Payment Terms (**Note:** Be aware of credit card fraud, www.cybersource.com)
- [ ] Regulatory documentation – Schedule B number
- [ ] Return policy
- [ ]

Note: Consider using a fulfillment center like www.bongous.com. These firms handle packaging, shipping, documentation and Export Regulation Administration requirements.

International Launch Plan Step #3

Estimate Foreign Market Landed Cost

The initial step in developing a local pricing model for a particular foreign market is to estimate the Landed Cost. The goal of the landed cost exercise is to be able to compare the Landed Cost of your product to the price of similar locally produced products or foreign competitors.

Essentially the Landed Cost calculation attempts to identify all costs associated with getting the product from the U.S. manufacturing facility to the door of the foreign buyer including logistics and import duties.

Final Landed Costs should be calculated only when all 8 steps have been addressed and with the assistance of a knowledgeable freight forwarder.

The following is an example of some of the hidden costs that need to be included in the total Landed Cost.

Line Cost Items	Cost
☐ CIF Calculations	
☐ Freight	
☐ Insurance	
Total CIF Price (cost, insurance, freight)	
Landing Charges	
☐ Import Duty	
☐ Port Costs	
☐ Warehousing and expediter	
☐ Terminal Handling Charges	
☐ Compulsory Contribution to Unions or Merchant Marine Taxes	
☐ Custom brokerage fee	
☐ Bank costs	
Total Landing Charges	
Total Landed Cost (local taxes and local distribution costs not included)	

Note: Import duties and line cost items are usually calculated based on a specific INCOTERM® of delivery (see Step #6: Transportation). The formula to estimate the cost to insure is usually CIF plus 110% (100% value +10% profit).

Example: Goods valued @ $12,000 + insurance@$1,000 + freight @ $2,000 = $15,000 CIF, Insure for $15,000 x 110%=$16,500

International Launch Plan Step #3

Additional Costs to Consider for Each Job

Please note that not every shipment will require all the components listed below and your calculation should <u>not</u> include domestic overhead costs.

Description	Cost
☐ Banking charges (service fees, interest, L/C, exchange rate, wire transfers)	
☐ Bid securities, performance or maintenance bonds for construction	
☐ Business travel	
☐ Consultants, on-site	
☐ Credit/background check for customer, partner, agent, distributor and other service providers	
☐ Entertainment/gifts NOT in violation of FCPA (customary to give token gifts based on company policy)	
☐ Freight - additional	
☐ Cargo insurance for merchandise replacement, damage, theft	
☐ Credit insurance for non-payment by foreign buyer	
☐ International postage for shipping samples, documents	
☐ Communications (international faxes, long distance, use Skype)	
☐ Market research (free or fee-based), job specific	
☐ Packaging to survive international journey and multiple handlings	
☐ Intellectual Property (copyright, patent, trademark filing, enforcement)	
☐ Testing for compliance to country-specific standards and registrations (CE mark, etc)	
☐ Pre-shipment inspections (SGS inspections)	
☐ Product or label modifications, size ingredients, language, measurement or metric	
☐ Documentation (Consular, notary, Chamber of Commerce, Certificate of Free Sale, etc)	
☐ Freight Forwarder fee	
☐ Supplemental cargo insurance	
☐ Translation (manuals, web, literature)	
☐ Legal (contract development and review, distributor)	
☐ Country-specific marketing	
☐ Sales commission	
☐ Volume discount	
☐ Training (SBDC, BIS, ITAR, etc), on-site, job specific	
☐ Licensing	

Pricing

There are many alternate ways to calculate your pricing structure, all of which take into account Landed Costs. This is your base point and your importer's starting point.

Leif Holmvall, author of *Export Pro*, states "The price of a product or service has to do with what the market is willing to pay plus the number of people on the 'journey' that have to make money. Thus the longer the distribution chain the higher the cost. It is not unusual to have several different country specific prices for the same item. The customer is only willing to pay a certain amount for an item. If there is a longer distribution chain they will not pay more, you will make less."

Although there are many alternatives, there are some firm rules to consider.
- Above all, research local market pricing comparisons to learn what the market will bear
- Do not duplicate domestic pricing less a discount
- Do not begin with manufacturing costs and randomly add on a markup
- Leave room for negotiation; it is a cultural must in some countries

International Launch Plan Step #4

Step #4: Legal

5 Ws of Legal

Why is this step important?
Internationally there are several, very different legal systems. Every company who operates internationally needs to address contract and Intellectual Property (IP) issues from an international and country-specific perspective.

What do you need to know?  **What** do you need to do?
(see checklist)

Contracts
- The governing legal systems, written and customary legal approaches for the country to which you are exporting
- The U.S. legal considerations when operating here and abroad
- Advice from a lawyer for the following red flags:
  - Include a contract clause that names the other party <u>only</u> as an independent contractor that carries NO legal rights
  - Watch out for distributor "exclusivity" clauses with the goal to thwart your product in favor of their main customer
  - A clear performance clause and exit clause

Intellectual Property (IP)
- The 4 types of intellectual property
- The status of IP protection in the prospective country
- What types of intellectual property protection you will pursue
- Costs to pursue international IP protection (current and in the future)
- Do not let anyone but you register your TM, otherwise you may not own your own name

Where do you go to find this information?
- www.exportlegal.org (ELAN) • www.export.gov (Country Commercial Guide)
- www.wipo.int   • www.stopfakes.gov   • www.ggmark.com
- www.sba.gov/content/small-business-development-centers-sbdcs/

Who can help you?
- 1-800-USA-TRAD(e) _____
- USEAC _____
- SBDC _____
- ELAN State Representative @ www.exportlegal.org _____
- Lawyer specializing in international contracts _____
- Lawyer specializing in international protection of IP _____

When should you perform tasks?

- ▸ Set up introductory appt with ELAN
- ▸ Determine the important provisions in the international contract
- ▸ If you haven't already done so, make an appointment with an IP lawyer
- ▸ Determine type, extent & cost of IP protection

- ▸ Refine and finalize contract with overseas partner(s)
- ▸ Finalize IP protection & strategy
- ▸ _____
- ▸ _____
- ▸ _____

ELAN – Export Legal Assistance Network, FCPA-Foreign Corrupt Practices Act, IP- Intellectual Property, OFAC-Office of Foreign Assets Control, PCT-Patent Cooperation Treaty, WIPO-World Intellectual Property Organization

2012 © Taranis, LLC

International Launch Plan Step #4

Step #4 Basics

Types of Legal Systems

There are different types of legal systems in the world that affect your contracts and relationships with distributors or sales agents. There are also U.S. laws that affect your business dealings abroad. Be informed! Find a lawyer with international, country specific expertise when writing international contracts.

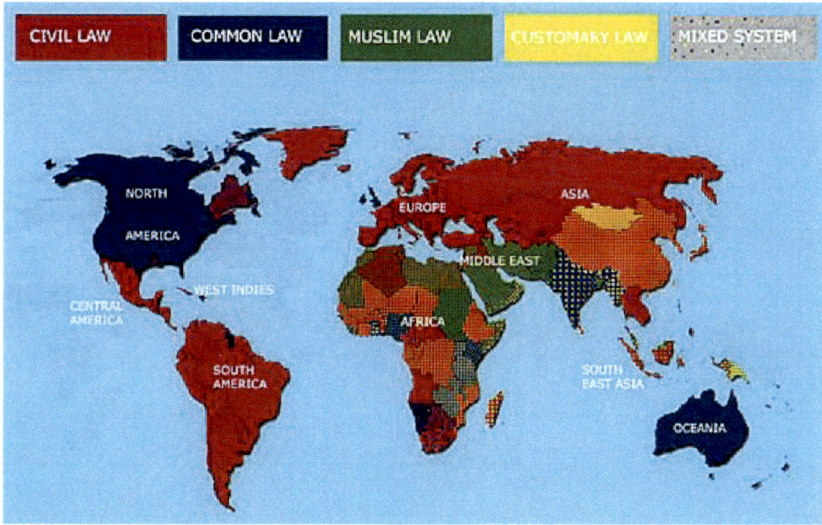

4 Types of Intellectual Property

- **Patents** are legal property rights applied to inventions. Typically, patents apply to such items as processes, machines, manufacturing designs, biological discoveries, or "compositions of matter."
- **Trade secrets** are practices, designs, formulas, processes, recipes, or ideas used by a company that allows it to gain leverage in its industry. Typically, trade secrets are kept hidden by one's own means, as opposed to being protected through government policies.
- **Trade Marks** include any words, phrases, symbols, logos, designs, or devices that are used in association with a particular brand or good in order to distinguish it from other products of that industry. Trademark protection is as important to your international development as a patent.
- **Copyrights** protect the original authors of both published and unpublished creations.

There is no such thing as an international patent. The PCT (Patent Cooperation Treaty) is like a reservation at your favorite restaurant. It holds your place in line and offers protection until you file in each individual country. Patent protection is time consuming, expensive and in some countries gives only limited protection.

2012 © Taranis, LLC

International Launch Plan Step #4

What You Need To Do Checklist

Contracts
- [ ] Determine the type of representative or partner that is best for your company, see pg. 31
  Note: Use the Selection Criteria for Overseas Partners in Step #2: Market Research pg. 20.
- [ ] Schedule a free introductory visit with ELAN, exportlegal.org (be prepared), see pg 31
- [ ] Identify the governing legal systems for the country to which you are exporting, the laws of payments in and out of the country and unwritten legal customs, see pg. 31
- [ ] Complete Contract Checklist, see pg. 32
- [ ] Cultural Communication affects every step of the eight-step process. What cultural issues should you consider with this step? (see Step #8)

Intellectual Property
- [ ] Determine level of IP protection in country of choice, see pg. 33
- [ ] Determine which of the 4 types of intellectual property protection you need, see pg. 33
- [ ] Find an Intellectual Property lawyer that has international expertise, see pg. 33
- [ ] Create an IP plan, see pg. 33
- [ ] Cultural Communication affects every step of the eight-step process. What cultural issues should you consider with this step? (see Step #8)

Legal Notes

International Launch Plan Step #4

Additional Forms

Note: Contracts will vary for each type of representative or partner.

Type of Representative/Partner That is Best for Your Company

Country you are exporting to _____

Type	Your Legal Responsibility	Required Documentation	How does this fit business model?	Ease of Termination
Employee in country				
Independent Sales Agent				
Distributor				
EMC/ETC				

Introductory Visit with ELAN and/or Contract Lawyer

Questions/Red Flags	Answers/Notes

Country you are exporting to _____

Questions	Answers/Notes
What is the governing legal system for this country?	
What are this country's laws on payments in and out of the country?	
Are there any unwritten legal customs in this country that you need to be aware of?	

International Launch Plan Step #4

Contract Check List Considerations

Using the criteria in Step #2: Market Research, establish the parameters for the contract with overseas partner(s). Contracts can be adjusted, depending on the choice of EMC, ETC, independent agent or distributor.

Note: Hiring an employee involves extensive research into the labor laws of the specific country. Contracts often require an attorney in the specified country.

General
- [ ] Clear introduction of all parties of the contract
- [ ] Territory- can be defined geographically, market segment, specific distribution channels or specific customer list
- [ ] Description of one or many product lines
- [ ] Exclusivity and restriction of sale of similar or competitive products
- [ ] Rights of the exporter in said territory
- [ ] Country of jurisdiction & governing law
- [ ] Contract language
- [ ] Ownership of all intellectual property
- [ ] Duration of the contract with extension provision
- [ ] Delivery and shipping terms
- [ ] Method and terms of payment
- [ ] Transfer title of goods
- [ ] Payment policy regarding commissions and payments
- [ ] Currency of payments and currency fluctuation clause

Duties of the Exporter
- [ ] Define the level of product quality and accompanying service support
- [ ] Marketing materials
- [ ] Delivery performance commitment
- [ ] Warranty, maintenance, liability duties

Status & Duties of the Distributor/Independent Sales Agent
- [ ] Clause defining the limited capabilities of the overseas partner as a representative not a legal agent
- [ ] Continued exclusivity from competitive products
- [ ] Level of service required
- [ ] Performance clauses
- [ ] Inventory Requirements
- [ ] Compliance with all U.S. laws (FCPA, Anti-Boycott) and Export Administration Regulations
- [ ] Marketing responsibilities
- [ ] Repair, maintenance and warranty responsibilities
- [ ] Training requirements
- [ ] Reporting obligations
- [ ] Process for new product introduction

Termination
- [ ] Grounds for termination
- [ ] Dispute settlement clause and country of jurisdiction
- [ ] Length of notice required for termination
- [ ] Consequences of termination
- [ ] Escape clauses for each party

2012 © Taranis, LLC

International Launch Plan Step #4

Level of IP Protection

Country governing body _____ (see Country Commercial Guide, Free Trade Agreements)
In country counsel _____

Level	Comments	Cost	Duration
☐ High			
☐ Medium			
☐ Low			

Type of IP Protection Required

Note: Often products and their brand require more than one form of IP protection.

4 IP Types	Initial Cost & Maintenance	Ability to protect	Duration
☐ Patent			
☐ Trademark			
☐ Copyright			
☐ Trade Secret			

Note: Make sure the trade secret information is secured in a safety deposit box.

Intellectual Property Lawyer Initial Meeting

🚩 Do not let anyone but you or your lawyer register your TM, otherwise you may not own your own name.

Questions	Answers/Notes

IP Plan

Action	Target Start Date	Target Completion Date
☐		
☐		
☐		
☐		

International Launch Plan Step #5

Step #5: Regulatory Compliance

5 Ws of Regulatory Compliance

Why is this step important?

As an exporter you are the USPPI (U.S. Principal Party of Interest) and it is your responsibility to determine if you need an export license and to follow all of the laws of the EAR (Export Administration Regulations).
Export Here = Import There, so you must meet import regulations required on the *other side of the ocean.*

What do you need to know?  **What** do you need to do?
(see checklist)

- You are responsible for determining if your product requires a license to export
- Regulatory compliance on the *other side of the ocean*
- How to determine if your product/order requires an export license
- When to call a regulatory compliance specialist
- What actions to take if a license is required
- What documentation must be submitted (see Step #6: Transportation)
- U.S. record keeping requires documents be maintained for five years
- Regulatory requirements *on the other side of the ocean*

-  BIS red flags www.bis.doc.gov/enforcement/redflags.htm

- Remember Export Here = Import There so start checking out import requirements and testing early in the game

Where do you go to find this information?
- www.export.gov   • www.bis.doc.gov   • www.csa-international.org
- www.bis.doc.gov/snap/index.htm (SNAP-R application)
- www.i-b-t.net (sign up for email Q & A)   • www.intertek.com/
- www.percept.com/product-regulatory-compliance/global-certification.html
- www.sba.gov/content/small-business-development-centers-sbdcs/

Who can help you?
- 1-800-USA-TRAD(e) _____
- USEAC _____
- BIS Regional Offices at (949) 660-0144 or (408) 998-8806
- Exporter Counseling Division at (202) 482-4811
- Regulatory Compliance Specialist _____

When should you perform tasks?

- ▸ Determine if your product needs a license, if so, contact an international regulatory compliance specialist
- ▸ Determine the country import requirements
- ▸ Meet with a Freight Forwarder (again) this time for assistance with outbound and inbound compliance regulations

- ▸ Set up your company's Export Compliance Manual
- ▸ Begin any foreign required testing or certifications
- ▸ _____
- ▸ _____

AES-Automated Export System, BIS-Bureau of Industry & Security, CCL-Commerce Control List, CCC-China Compulsory Certification, CCC-County Control Chart, CE-Conformité Européen, EAR-Export Administration Regulations, EAR-99, ECCN-Export Control Classification Number, EEI-Electronic Export Information, FCPA-Foreign Corrupt Practices Act, ITAR-International Traffic in Arms Regulations, ITN-Internal Transaction Number, MRA-Mutually Recognized Agreement, NLR-No License Required, OFAC-Office of Foreign Asset Control, RoHS-Restriction of Hazardous Substances, Schedule B, SED-Shipper's Export Declaration, SDN-Specially Designated National, USPPI-U.S. Principal Party of Interest, WEEE-Waste of Electrical & Electronic Equipment

2012 © Taranis, LLC

International Launch Plan Step #5

Step #5 Basics

Who Controls Export?

 U.S. State Department-Directorate of Defense Trade Controls (DDTC)-defense articles & services, ITAR

 Commerce Department-Bureau of Industry and Security (BIS)-"dual use" items, EAR

 Treasury Department-Office of Foreign Assets Control (OFAC) oversees embargo and sanction lists

 Department of Homeland Security- Customs and Border Protection (CBP) enforces all exports at U.S. borders.

 Bureau of Census-trade-statistics and the AES

Regulations for exports are known as the **EAR** (Export Administration Regulations)

3 types of exports

- Tangible - shipped through a US port via air, ocean, rail or truck

- Intangible - through email, technical drawings or someone's brain ("deemed exports")

- Re-Exports - shipments from one foreign country to another of US origin goods or foreign made goods containing certain US origin parts, components or materials

Do I need a license? Ask the following 4 questions.

- What is the product (commercial or potential military use)?
- Who is buying the product?
- Where is it going?
- How will it be used?

Note: You are the USPPI (U.S. Principal Party of Interest) AND it is your responsibility to determine if your order needs a license. Only 5 % of items require a license. Those that do not need a license, use the ECCN (Export Control Classification Number) of EAR-99 when filing documents. Those items that might need a license need to complete the 7 step process, determine the ECCN, obtain a license and file the necessary documents. Every company should maintain an Export Compliance Manual tracking the products' security risk from cradle to grave.

Testing/Certification

 There are many possible legal and certification requirements for your product. Check out your country of export, determine these requirements and begin the testing/certification process as soon as possible.

2012 © Taranis, LLC

International Launch Plan Step #5

What You Need to Do Checklist

- [ ] Determine the type of export, see pg. 37
- [ ] Answer 4 questions to determine if your product needs a license, see pg. 37
  If so, hire an international regulatory compliance lawyer to assist in determination of the ECCN, export license and filing of SNAP-R.
- [ ] Go through the 7 steps to finalize license requirements and determine ECCN number, see pg. 37-39
- [ ] Create an Export Compliance Manual using the mandatory 9 components, see pg. 39 and Appendix C
- [ ] Determine the country import requirements and product requirements necessary to import into the country of choice, see pg. 41
- [ ] Determine any foreign required testing or certifications, see pg. 41
- [ ] Cultural Communication affects every step of the eight-step process. What cultural issues should you consider with this step?
  (see Step #8)

Regulatory Compliance Notes

International Launch Plan Step #5

Additional Forms

Type of Export

Type	Product A	Product B	Product C
Tangible - Shipments through a U.S. port via air, ocean, rail, truck or via mail			
Intangible 1 - Electronic transfers, email, downloads			
Intangible 2 - Technical reports, drawings released to foreign nationals			
Intangible 3 - "Deemed Exports" information seen or learned while a foreign national is visiting your facility			
Re-Export - Shipments of products of US origin from one foreign country to another			

4 Questions to Determine if You Need a License

Questions	Product A	Product B	Product C
1. What?			
2. Who?			
3. Where?			
4. End Use?			

7 Steps to Complete License Requirements

See http://www.bis.doc.gov/licensing/exportingbasics.htm

1. **Know & classify your item**
   Technical products may require assistance from an engineer or the U.S. Census Commodity Branch at 1-800-549-0595.
   Note: If your item falls under ITAR (International Traffic in Arms Regulation) you are using the wrong book.
2. **Check if your item is on the CCL (Commerce Control List) Alphabetical Index**
   See http://www.bis.doc.gov/policiesandregulations/ear/ccl_index.pdf
   This Index will give you the ECCN (Export Control Classification Number).

   Example: Polygraphs……………………………………3A981

   If the item is listed, [STOP], hire a regulatory compliance specialist and continue to #3.

   If it is not listed, go to #5.

2012 © Taranis, LLC

International Launch Plan Step #5

3. **Determine the reason for a license or if there are exceptions to a license**
   Return to the CCL, this time to the category listing at
   http://www.bis.doc.gov/policiesandregulations/ear/index.htm

   In the example of the Polygraph Equipment (3A981), the Category is 3: Electronics, and the License Requirements and License Exceptions listed are CC (Crime Control).

   License Requirements may include:
   - AT (Anti-Terrorism)
   - CB (Chemical & Biological Weapons)
   - CC (Crime Control)
   - NS (National Security)
   - MT (Missile Technology)
   - NP (Nuclear Non-Proliferation)
   - RS (Regional Stability)
   - UN (United Nations Embargo)

   License Exceptions may include:
   - CIV (Civil End Users)
   - BAG (Baggage)
   - GFT (Gift & Humanitarian Donation)
   - LVS (Limited Value Shipment)
   - TMP (Temporary Import, Export Re-Export)

4. **Cross check the ECCN with the CCC (Commerce Country Chart)**
   See http://www.bis.doc.gov/policiesandregulations/ear/738_supp1.pdf

   Cross check the reason against the country of export.
   - An X means a license is required
   - No X means NLR (no license required)

   Example: Polygraphs

   ### Commerce Country Chart
   #### Reason for Control

Countries	Chemical & Biological Weapons			Nuclear Nonproliferation		National Security		Missile Tech	Regional Stability		Firearms Convention	Crime Control		
	CB 1	CB 2	CB 3	NP 1	NP 2	NS 1	NS 2	MT 1	RS 1	RS 2	FC 1	CC 1	CC 2	CC 3
Guyana	X	X		X		X		X	X	X	X	X		X
Haiti	X	X		X		X		X	X	X	X	X		X
Honduras	X	X		X		X		X	X	X	X	X		X
Hong Kong	X	X		X		X			X	X		X		X
Hungary	X					X	X	X	X					
Iceland	X			X		X	X	X	X					
India	X	X	X	X	X	X	X	X	X	X		X		X

International Launch Plan Step #5

5. **Check the lists that show prohibited parties to export to**
   See http://www.bis.doc.gov/complianceandenforcement/liststocheck.htm
   - Denied Persons
   - Unverified List
   - Entity List
   - SDN (Specially Designated Nationals)
   - Debarred List
   - Nonproliferation Sanctions
   or
   - Consolidated Screening List
     (http://export.gov/ecr/eg_main_023148.asp)

6. **For products that require a license, apply through SNAP-R**
   - Any product requiring a license (SNAP-R) must file an EEI (Electronic Export Information) with the AES (Automated Export System)
   - See http://www.bis.doc.gov/snap/index.htm

7. **File EEI with AES (if applicable AES 1-Rule)**
   See Step #6: Transportation. Your freight forwarder can file this for you.

   Filing your EEI with the AES
   AES 1 RULE
   - **One** USPPI shipping their merchandise to
   - **One** foreign consignee on
   - **One** carrier moving the product out of the U.S. on
   - **One** day
   - Valued at over $2,500 per Schedule B number or when a license is required

   Remember
   - A product not requiring a license is considered NLR and uses EAR-99 in the box for the ECCN #
   - Any export requiring a license MUST file an EEI regardless of value

International Launch Plan Step #5

Do you need a license?

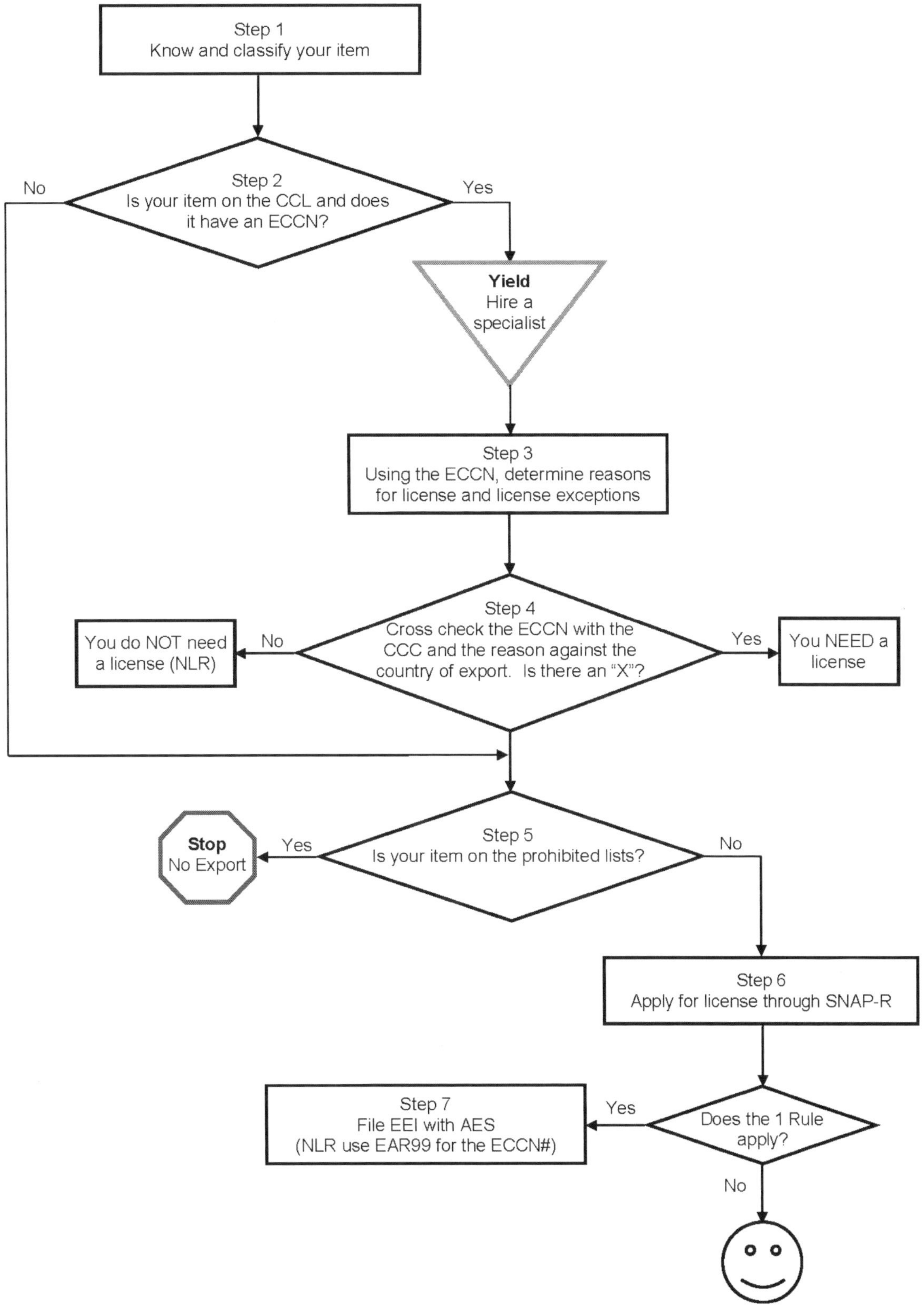

```
Step 1
Know and classify your item
   │
   ▼
Step 2 ── Yes ──▶ Yield: Hire a specialist
Is your item on the CCL              │
and does it have an ECCN?            ▼
   │                          Step 3
   No                         Using the ECCN, determine reasons
   │                          for license and license exceptions
   │                                  │
   │                                  ▼
   │     ┌── No ── Step 4 ── Yes ──▶ You NEED a license
   │     ▼          Cross check the ECCN with the
   │  You do NOT   CCC and the reason against the
   │  need a       country of export. Is there an "X"?
   │  license
   │  (NLR)
   │                                  │
   └──────────────────────────────────┤
                                      ▼
       Stop ◀── Yes ── Step 5
       No Export       Is your item on the prohibited lists?
                                      │ No
                                      ▼
                            Step 6
                            Apply for license through SNAP-R
                                      │
                                      ▼
       Step 7           ◀── Yes ── Does the 1 Rule apply?
       File EEI with AES                │
       (NLR use EAR99 for the ECCN#)    No
                                        ▼
                                       :-)
```

2012 © Taranis, LLC

International Launch Plan Step #5

Export Compliance Manual

An Export Compliance Manual must contain the following 9 key components. For an example, see Appendix C.

☐	1.	Management commitment
☐	2.	Risk analysis
☐	3.	Export Compliance Manual Policy - information gathered & action required on each initial transaction
☐	4.	Proof of training
☐	5.	Cradle to grave export compliance security
☐	6.	Recordkeeping
☐	7.	Export compliance monitoring & audit
☐	8.	Problems
☐	9.	Correct action(s) or policy or if applicable

Regulatory Compliance on the Other Side of the Ocean

Legal requirements to do business (see Step #4: Legal):

Import requirements:

Label conversion and translation:

Product standards or licensing requirements:

Testing Results or Requirements (see testing agencies under "Who Can Help You"):
  Note: In some cases, countries accept MRA (Mutual Recognition Agreements). More often the product requires testing by a certified agency to meet country-specific standards.

Required marks like CE, UL, FCC (see www.electrosuisse.ch/certification/global_product_approval_E.htm):

International Launch Plan Step #6

Step #6: Transportation

5 Ws of Transportation

Why is this step important?

Goods held up on the dock or in foreign country customs, NO GOODS, NO PAY
Goods damaged in transit, NO GOODS, NO PAY
Incorrect documents, NO GOODS, NO PAY
Ship goes down and you have no insurance, not only NO GOODS, NO PAY but you are responsible for the entire cargo's value.
These are only some of the reasons why your Freight Forwarder is your BFF!

What do you need to know?  **What** do you need to do?
(see checklist)

- Freight Forwarders and how they differ from Customs Brokers
- When to contact a Freight Forwarder (Step #3 Market Entry for Landed Costs)
- How to choose a Freight Forwarder that is a good match for you
- What are INCOTERMS® and how they affect your level of obligation and risk
- International transport analysis & cost comparison
- When to use small shipment carriers
- What documents and filings are required for your shipment (see Appendix D)
- GOODS= DOCS=MONEY
- Why insurance is essential
- Shipment to trade shows: ATA Carnets

- INSURANCE, INSURANCE and don't forget the INSURANCE (even when the INCOTERMS® specify other party payment, buy supplemental insurance)

Where do you go to find this information?
- www.americanshipper.com • www.azfreight.com • www.forwarders.com
- www.worldportsource.com/index.php • www.findaport.net • www.ups.com
- www.transport911.com • www.oceanschedules.com
- www.zurichna.com (view interactive white paper) • www.freightquote.com/
- www.onlineconversion.com • www.apx-air-cargo.com • www.fedex.com
- www.shippingandfreightresource.com/
- www.chrobinson.com/en/us/Global-Services/Global-Trade-Resources
- www.aphis.usda.gov/import_export/plants/plant_exports/wpm/wpm_faqs.shtml#1

Who can help you?
- 1-800-USA-TRAD(e) _____
- USEAC _____
- SBDC _____
- Local customs broker and freight forwarders association _____

When should you perform tasks?

- Create Power of Attorney for freight forwarder
- Know your level of obligation of the INCOTERM® listed in your contract
- Verify documentation info for Freight Forwarder

- If using an LC, confirm freight forwarder has LC expertise
- Re-evaluate your shipping options if necessary & finalize your logistics plan

AES-Automated Export System, BL-Bill of Lading, COO-Certificate of Origin, EEI - Electronic Export Information, FCL/LCL-Full Container Load & Less Than Container Load, SED-Shipper's Export Declaration, TEU/FEU-20' equivalent unit & 40' equivalent unit, ULD-Unit Loading Device, USPPI-U.S. Principal Party of Interest, INCOTERMS = EXW-Ex Works, FCA-Free Carrier, FAS-Free Alongside Ship, FOB-Free On Board, CFR-Cost & Freight, CIF-Cost, Insurance & Freight, CPT-Carriage Paid To, CIP-Carriage, Insurance Paid To, DAP-Delivered at Place, DAT-Delivered at Terminal, DDP-Delivered Duty Paid

2012 © Taranis, LLC

International Launch Plan Step #6

Step #6 Basics

Four Modes of Transportation

- Air
- Ocean
- Rail
- Truck

Multi-modal transportation is a combination

Freight Forwarders

Finding a good Freight Forwarder is ESSENTIAL!!! They will be your BFF!

INCOTERMS®

The INCOTERMS® 2010 dictates your level of obligation and risk in the transportation of your goods from you to your client. Be informed!!

Documentation...always remember

The Goods   The Docs   The Money

For trade shows use an **ATA Carnet**. It is your product's passport that allows you to bring your product into a country for a short amount of time without paying import duties.

Insurance, insurance and don't forget the insurance

2012 © Taranis, LLC

International Launch Plan Step #6

What You Need to Do Checklist

- ☐ Questionnaire for Choosing a Freight Forwarder, see pg. 45
- ☐ Transportation Analysis, see pg. 46
- ☐ Packaging and Unique Transportation Issues, see pg. 46
- ☐ Small Shipments, see pg. 47
- ☐ INCOTERMS®, see pg. 48
- ☐ Documents, see pg. 49 and Appendix D
- ☐ Insurance, see pg. 49
- ☐ Cultural Communication affects every step of the eight-step process. What cultural issues should you consider with this step? (see Step #8)

Transportation Notes

International Launch Plan Step #6

Additional Forms

Questionnaire for Choosing a Freight Forwarder

	Questions to Ask	Comments
☐	1. Does the Freight Forwarder deal with newbies? Are they willing to educate you?	
☐	2. Is the Freight Forwarder small enough to handle your projects personally BUT has a sufficient support staff worldwide?	
☐	3. Does the Freight Forwarder have a large network of good agents in the overseas market you are dealing with? (vital for perishable products)	
☐	4. Does the Freight Forwarder have experience in all four methods of shipment- air, ocean, rail and truck?	
☐	5. What are the Freight Forwarders product specialties? Do they have geographic, market or industry specialization? Do they have expertise in handling your product? Do they have the expertise if it requires special provisions such as refrigeration?	
☐	6. Is the freight forwarder licensed or approved by the appropriate entities? (In the United States, ocean freight forwarders must be licensed by the Federal Maritime Commission to handle ocean cargo. Although not legally required, the International Air Transport Association (IATA) registers freight forwarders to deal with international air cargo shipments.)	
☐	7. Do they offer a full line of related services, such as customs house brokerage, insurance, documentation support and various transportation options? Customs brokerage is essential if items are returned.	
☐	8. Will they be able to answer your quotation inquiries within 48 hours?	
☐	9. What is the Freight Forwarder's turnaround time for documentation?	
☐	10. Does the Freight Forwarder demonstrate knowledge of U.S. government export regulations?	
☐	11. Are they financially sound? Does the Freight Forwarder have "errors and omissions" insurance?	
☐	12. Do they give dependable and competitive quotations of freight cost, port charges, consular and handling fees? Are their quotes broken down and clearly understood?	
☐	13. Does the company have the capability to track and trace goods worldwide?	
☐	14. Will a specific person be assigned to oversee and manage your account?	
☐	15. Does the firm have experience in consolidating freight for shipping?	
☐	16. Will the company develop creative, competitive and customized services for its clients? Can they assist you with packing or refer you to someone.	

International Launch Plan Step #6

Transportation Analysis

Starting Point of Export _____

Ending Point of Delivery _____

- Is this a single mode of transportation or multi-modal? _____
- Can the shipment be containerized? _____
- Is it an FCL (Full Container Load) or must it be consolidated in an LCL (Less than Container Load) _____
- Are there any transportation restrictions or prohibitions for your product? _____
- Is your item considered HAZMAT? _____

Mode	Delivery Time	Cost (including surcharges)	Temperature or special conditions required	Restricted or Hazardous	Fragile	Size of Packaged Product	Infrastructure of Import Country
Air							
Ocean							
Rail							
Truck							

Packaging and Unique Transportation Issues

1. Packaging for all types of unknown conditions is essential.
2. Does the shipment require a specialized transport container such as refrigerated, insulated or ventilated, open top etc?
   _____

3. Who will handle the packaging, marking, shipper's letter of instruction?
   _____

4. **Theft Warning:** Do not label content for expensive items like iPhones or Nike shoes.
5. What special packaging and marking considerations apply to your product or shipment?
   Example: Chocolate cannot sit on the 110° tarmac at DFW Airport, computer parts are fragile and certain products require HAZMAT labeling and packaging.
   _____
   _____
   _____
   _____

International Launch Plan Step #6

Small Shipments

Small shipment carriers, also called integrated shippers, are fine for samples and small, initial shipments however they can be expensive. The USPS has the least expensive program and guarantees delivery to over 190 countries. **Note:** The post office on the other side of the ocean has to be good for USPS to work well.

Method	Pros	Cons	Costs
USPS (Country-specific max weight limits range from 22 - 70 pounds)			
FedEx			
UPS			

International Launch Plan Step #6

INCOTERMS®

As the exporter you are required to properly package the goods and prepare the export documentation. What matching INCOTERM® best fits your level of responsibility and risk? What additional level of responsibility are you willing to assume in order to deliver the product to your buyer?

- ☐ Inland Freight to US port
- ☐ Terminal Charges
- ☐ Loading on Vessel
- ☐ Delivery to Destination
- ☐ Insurance
- ☐ Arrival Charges
- ☐ Duty & taxes
- ☐ Inland Freight to client

Incoterms	EXW	FAS	FCA	FOB	CFR	CIF	CPT	CIP	DAT	DAP	DDP
Load to truck											
Export- duty payment											
Transport to exporter's port											
Unload from truck at the origin's port											
Landing charges at origin's port											
Transport to importer's port											
Landing charges at importer's port											
Unload onto trucks from the importers' port											
Transport to destination											
Insurance											
Entry - Customs clearance, Duties and Taxes											

■ Seller   ■ Buyer

2012 © Taranis, LLC

International Launch Plan Step #6

Documents

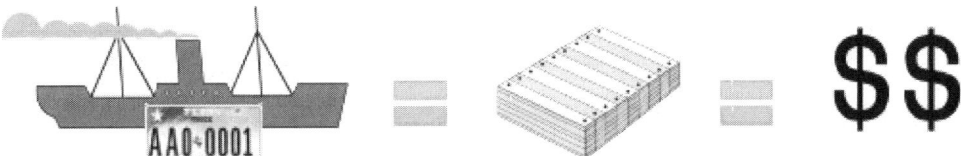

The Goods = The Docs = The Money

Required Documents	Additional Documents (if applicable)
☐ Proforma Invoice	☐ Certificate of Origin
☐ Commercial Invoice	☐ Consular Invoice Notarized
☐ Export Packing List	☐ Certificate of Free Sale
☐ SED/EEI	☐ Hazardous Goods Certificate
☐ Shipper's Letter of Instructions	☐ Health Certificate
☐ Bill of Lading-Ocean- Negotiable Doc	☐ Ingredients Certificate or Analysis
Air/Rail/Truck- Non Negotiable Doc	☐ Fumigation Certificate
☐ Export License	☐ Fisheries Certificate
☐ Destination Control Statement on Commercial Invoices, Ocean BOL, Air Waybill: *"THESE COMMODITIES, TECHNOLOGY OR SOFTWARE WERE EXPORTED FROM THE UNITED STATES IN ACCORDANCE WITH THE EXPORT ADMINISTRATION REGULATIONS. DIVERSION CONTRARY TO U.S. LAW PROHIBITED."*	☐ Halal Certificate ☐ Phytosanitary Certificate ☐ Radiation Certificate ☐ Inspection Certificates ☐ Import License ☐ Weight Certificate ☐ ISMP 15 Certificate ☐ ATA Carnet for trade shows

Insurance

Type	Coverage Pros/Cons	Cost
All Risk		
Shipment by Shipment		
CIF		
Umbrella Policies		

Note: The formula to estimate the cost to insure is usually CIF plus 110% (100% value +10% profit). Example: Goods valued @ $12,000 + insurance@$1,000 + freight@$2,000 = $15,000 CIF, Insure for $15,000 x 110%=$16,500

International Launch Plan Step #7

Step #7: Payments/Finance

5 Ws of Payments/Finance

Why is this step important?
Doing business internationally involves additional risk. Every exporter should be aware of the types of risk, analyze the risk and take steps to minimize the risk.
Knowing the pros/cons of the different types of payment methods allows an exporter to make an informed decision on the preferred method of payment.

What do you need to know?      **What** do you need to do?
(see checklist)

- The importance of working with a bank/banker who has expertise in international transactions and is an approved SBA or EX-IM bank lender
- Types of risk
- Types of payments
- Use a risk analysis flow chart for evaluation
- Available services, public and private, to minimize risk
- Government finance assistance programs and tax incentives
- Revising and expanding your risk management policy
- NEVER do business with anyone until you have checked their financial credit

Where do you go to find this information?
- www.duke.edu/~charvey/Country_risk/couindex.htm
- www.coface.com   • www.oecd.org   • www.fas.usda.gov/
- www.export.gov/salesandmarketing/eg_main_018198.asp
- www.dnb.com   • www.fitchratings.com/
- www.graydon.co.uk   • www.owens.com/
- www.creditworthy.com/providers/collection_f.html
- www.gtnews.com/risk/default.cfm?s2=67
- www.exim.gov   • www.transparency.org/   • www.worldbank.org/
- www.sba.gov/category/navigation-structure/exporting-importing
- www.susta.org/services/map_faq.html
- www.sba.gov/content/small-business-development-centers-sbdcs/

Who can help you?
- 1-800-USA-TRAD(e) _____
- USEAC _____
- International SBA rep_____
- Regional EX-IM Bank rep_____
- WTC, EDA or local trade alliance _____

When should you perform tasks?

▸ Analyze country risk
▸ Complete customer credit check
▸ Determine if SBA or EX-IM Bank programs are a good fit. If so, begin the application process.

▸ Consider FX hedging
▸ Start molding your future risk management strategy
▸ _____
▸ _____

Sidebar: Anti-boycott language, ICP-International Company Profile, LC-Letter of Credit, LC Terms: Seller=Exporter=Drawer=Beneficiary, Buyer=Importer=Drawee=Applicant, Banks=Advising or Confirming Bank, OPIC-Overseas Private Investment Corporation, SDN-Specially Designated National, SWIFT-Society for Worldwide Interbank Financial Telecommunication

2012 © Taranis, LLC

International Launch Plan Step #7

Step #7 Basics

It's All About Risk

3 Main Types of Risk
- Company

- Political

- FX (Foreign Exchange)

4 Main Types of Payments with Varying Levels of Risk for the Exporter

- Cash in Advance
- Letter of Credit
- Documentary Collection
- Open Account

Payment Procedures

Least Risk

Cash in Advance

Letter of Credit
Commercial or Standby
Confirmed or Advised

Documentary Collection
On sight
Time Draft

Open Account

Highest Risk

Opportunities to Minimize Risk

- Working Capital
- Medium Term Loans
- Export Credit Insurance

Available through

- Small Business Administration
- Export-Import Bank of the United States
- Private Banks

International Launch Plan Step #7

What You Need to Do Checklist

- [ ] Interview Questions for Your Bank, see pg. 53
- [ ] Country Risk and Political Risk Analysis, see pg. 53
- [ ] Country Specific Policies on Payment Procedures, see pg. 54
- [ ] Individual Company Risk, see pg. 54
- [ ] FX Risk, see pg. 55
- [ ] Payment Risk Options, see pg. 56
- [ ] Do You Qualify as an IC-DISC?, see pg. 56
- [ ] 3 Types of government financial assistance
    - Export Development and Working Capital Financing, see pg. 57
    - Facilities Development Financing, see pg. 57
    - Financing for your International Buyers, see pg. 57
- [ ] Risk Analysis Flow Chart, see pg. 58
- [ ] Cultural Communication affects every step of the eight-step process. What cultural issues should you consider with this step? (see Step #8)

Payments/Finance Notes

International Launch Plan Step #7

Additional Forms

Interview Questions for Your Bank

Source: Melinda Barnes, Vice President, Wells Fargo HSBC Trade Bank

Question to ask	Yes	No	Comments
1. Does your bank deal in international transactions? If so, how long?			
2. Do you have branches or affiliate banks in other countries? If so, where?			
3. Do you have an international presence in my particular market?			
4. Do you have international payment procedures? If so what are they?			
5. Do you have expertise in international Letters of Credit?			
6. Do you know the country specific banking conditions in my particular market?			
7. Can you help educate me (with personal knowledge or advisory reports) on the banking conditions in my particular market?			
8. Are you knowledgeable on trade financing and foreign exchange issues for the small exporter?			
9. Do you have a working relationship with the SBA International Division and Ex-Im Bank?			

Country Risk and Political Risk

Country of export: _____

Type of Risk	Low	Medium	High	Comments/Concerns
Country				
Political				

Sources
- www.globaledge.msu.edu
- www.duke.edu/~charvey/Country_risk/couindex.htm
- www.coface.com
- www.oecd.org

International Launch Plan Step #7

Country Specific Policies on Payment Procedures

_____
_____
_____
_____
_____

Source
- www.export.gov (Country Commercial Guide)

Individual Company Risk

Ratings used are market conventions from AAA-BBB ("investment grade") to BB-D ("speculative grade"). They do not signify investment strategy but show the level of risk.
- AAA-BBB= low to moderate risk
- BB-D= higher level of credit risk or that a default has occurred.

Ratings vary slightly for the big three rating agencies: Fitch, Moody's and Standard & Poors.

Company Name	Credit Rating	Comments/concerns

Sources
- www.dnb.com (Dun & Bradstreet)
- www.fitchratings.com/ (Fitch, Inc.)
- www.graydon.co.uk (Graydon, UK)
- www.owens.com/ (Owens, Inc.)
- www.creditworthy.com/providers/collection_f.html (Credit Worthy listing of credit agencies by country)
- US Export Assistance Center International Company Profile report
- www.en.wikipedia.org/wiki/List_of_countries_by_credit_rating

International Launch Plan Step #7

FX Risk

Country _____

Note: A qualified international banker can advise you on foreign exchange risk management.

Currency	Recent Stability	Historic Stability	Range of Fluctuations	Comments/ Concerns	Options to manage

Current events which might suddenly affect currency or range of fluctuations:
_____
_____
_____
_____

Source
- www.gtnews.com/risk/default.cfm?s2=67

Some options to manage foreign exchange risk
- Spot market rate: price in foreign currency but demand cash in advance at today's exchange rate
- Net out foreign currency receipts with foreign currency expenditures
- Hedging - Forward Contract: enables exporter to sell a set amount of foreign currency at a pre-agreed exchange rate within the delivery date of the product
- Hedging - Options: similar to above, except it enables the exporter to acquire the right but not the obligation to deliver an agreed amount of foreign currency.

Note: Factoring and forfeiting are universally accepted as financial tools in certain international industries.

International Launch Plan Step #7

Payment Risk Options

Type	Level of Risk to You	$ Amt at Risk	Time of Collection	Level & Cost of Implementation	Compromise with buyer *
Cash Advance					
Cash Against Docs					
Docs Against Acceptance					
Letter of Credit					
Open Account					

* Most buyers want longer terms and to trade in their own currency

Letter of Credit questions to ask
- When is it advisable to use an LC?
- Who pays for the LC?
- LC cost vs your risk tolerance?
- What about amendments or stale docs?
- Are there any prohibited clauses in the LC such an anti-boycott clauses?
- Who pays for the Inspection?

Note: SGS (Societé Generale de Surveillance) Testing/Inspection Services will inspect anything, anywhere; quality and count. SGS certifications are recognized by most worldwide banks as bonafide documents.

Do You Qualify as an IC-DISC?
IC-DISC (Interest Charge - Domestic International Sales Corporation)
- Source: Dan Snyder, Weaver LLP, www.weaverllp.com/Services/TaxAndStrategic/IntConsulting/ICDISC.aspx

Criteria	Yes	No	Considering
Separate, domestic corporation w/$2500 capitalization			
Formally elect to be treated as an IC-DISC			
Must maintain separate bank account & accounting books			
Must file U.S. tax return even though it owes no taxes			

International Launch Plan Step #7

3 Types of Government Financial Assistance

Export Development and Working Capital

Examine your needs to determine your options for payment assistance and financing.
- EWCP - Export Working Capital Program
- STEP - State Trade and Export Promotion
- MAP - Market Access Program for branding and label reimbursement

Agency	Program	Approved Lender or Organization	Comments
SBA	EWCP		
SBA	Export Express		
SBA	STEP Grant		
EX-IM	EWCP		
FAS	MAP		
Bank/Outside Lender			

Facilities Development Financing

Agency	Program	Approved Lender or Organization	Comments
SBA	International Trade Loan Program		
Bank/Outside Lender			

Financing for your International Buyers

Agency	Program	Approved Lender or Organization	Comments
EX-IM	Single Buyer Credit Ins.		
EX-IM	Multi Buyer Credit Ins.		
EX-IM	Med Term Credit Ins.		Capital goods
EX-IM	Med/Long Terms Loan Guarantee		
EX-IM	Lease Guarantee		
FAS	GSM-102		

International Launch Plan Step #7

Risk Analysis Flow Chart

Risk Analysis Flowchart

Category	Options	Guidance	Outcome
Cargo & Risk Insurance	Yes!		You will sleep better at night
Export Credit Insurance	Single Buyer, Multi Buyer, Medium & Long Term Loan Guarantees	Start with single buyer. As you expand, move into more complex and extensive credit insurance programs	
Payment Options	Cash in Advance, Documentary Collection, Letter of Credit (LC), Open Credit		Start with cash in advance or documentary collections. Then with established relationship move to more open terms. For orders over $25K consider a LC or confirmed LC for highest security.
FX Risk	Low, Medium, High, Volatile	Start with US dollars. Expand FX Policy: • Non-hedging – Spot market rate – Net out foreign currency with foreign receivables • Hedging – Forward Contract – Options	
Company Credit Check	ICP or other credit check		What $ amount are you willing to risk with what payment terms?
Country Risk	Low, Medium, High, Volatile	Stay current on current events	
$ Amount of Order	$		Control risk with less risky payment terms
Expertise	NTE, NTM, NTC, Experienced	New to Export, New to Market, New to Client, Experienced	

2012 © Taranis, LLC

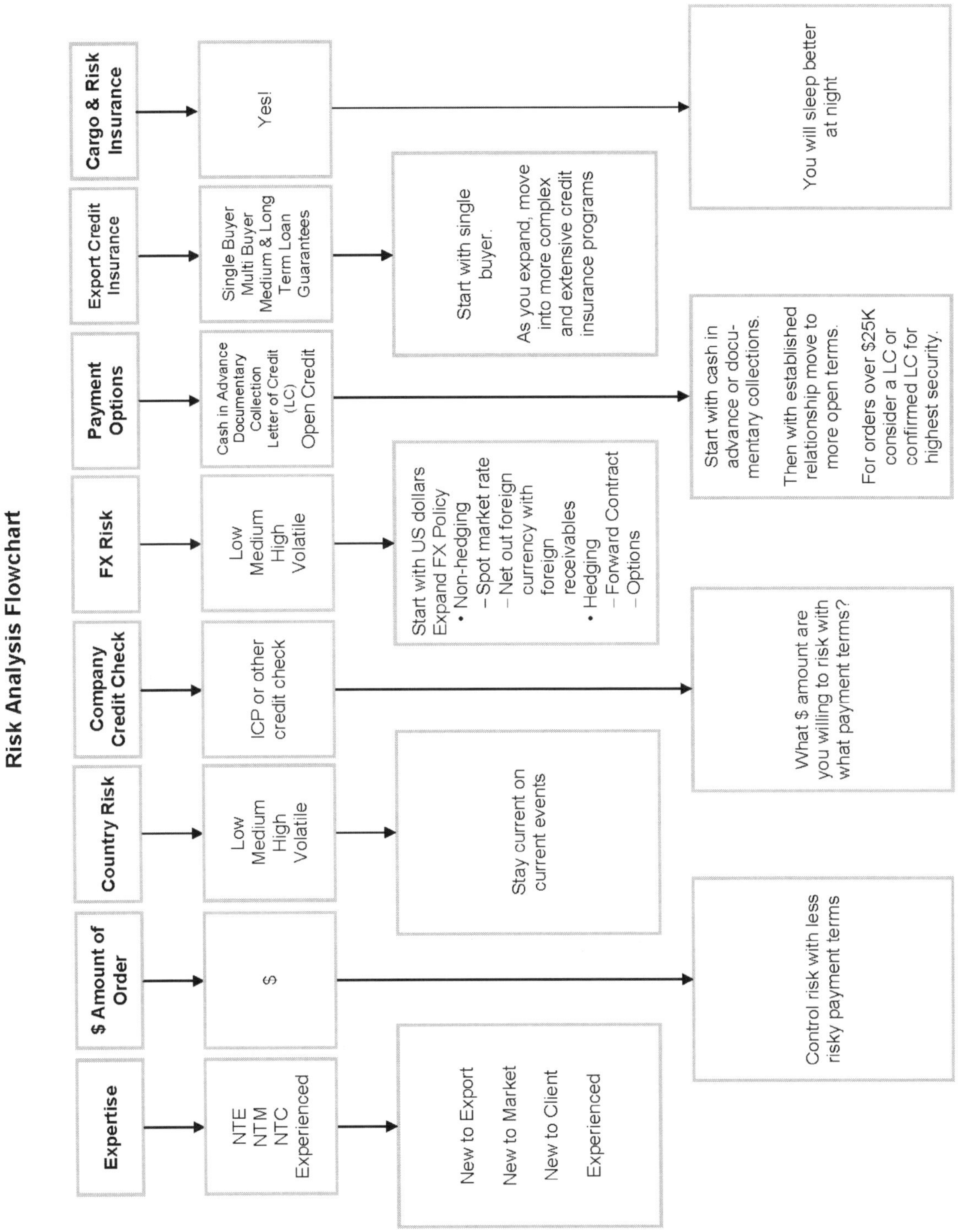

International Launch Plan Step #8

Step #8: Cultural

5 Ws of Cultural

"Don't Flunk Lunch"

Why is this step important?
Cultural Communications can (and usually do) make or break the deal in the beginning, the middle or the end.

What do you need to know?  **What do you need to do?**
(see checklist)

- Cultural communication affects every step of your international transaction
- 80% of your international success is determined by effective cultural communications and building good working relationships
- Cultural communications begin with your very first contact either via email, phone or in person
- Response to time, groups and hierarchy are very different in other cultures
- Customs vary regarding business meeting protocol, entertaining & negotiations
- Cultural communications don't stop when the contract is signed, they have only just begun

Where do you go to find this information?
- www.globaledge.msu.edu (videos and country indices)
- www.culturecrossing.net
- www.kwintessential.co.uk
- www.worldbusinessculture.com
- www.globalnegotiationresources.com (Lothar Katz)
- www.sba.gov/content/small-business-development-centers-sbdcs/

Who can help you?
- USEAC _____
- SBDC _____
- Local College Courses or Professors _____
- Private Consultants with in-country experience _____

When should you perform tasks?

- Research customs before contact
- Print new international business cards
- At a minimum, take a course at your local college
- Consider hiring a consultant with country expertise

- Be prepared to follow proper cultural protocol when you meet in person
- Know cultural negotiation style prior to contract negotiations
- Cultural communication is ongoing

2012 © Taranis, LLC

International Launch Plan Step #8

Step #8 Basics

Product	10%	**Success**	Product	40%	
Company	10%		Company	40%	
Cultural Communications	80%	**Failure**	Cultural Communications	20%	

Ways that Cultural Communication Affects International Business Relationships
- Religious customs that influence laws
- Direct or indirect communications styles
- Hierarchy in corporate cultures
- Negotiation tactics
- Decision-making
- Importance of masculinity vs. femininity
- Personal space and contact
- Attitude about time
- Customs regarding business entertaining and their influence on "making the deal"
- Meeting protocol
- Business Cards
- Respect for age
- Dress

What you think you know is only the tip of the iceberg.

"In rapport, all things are possible.
Out of rapport, nothing is possible."
                                                    E. Rice

International LAUNCH Plan Step #8

What You Need to Do Checklist
- [ ] Find a consultant who is an expert in this country's customs to help you with all of the items below
- [ ] Country Cultural Research, see pg. 62
- [ ] Business Cards, see pg. 62
- [ ] Proper Protocol or Custom for Business Meetings, see pg. 63
- [ ] Proper Protocol or Custom for Social Entertaining, see pg. 63
- [ ] Taboos and Deal Breakers, see pg. 64
- [ ] Negotiations, see pg. 64

Cultural Notes

International Launch Plan Step #8

Additional Forms

Country Cultural Research

Country _____

Item	Answer
Language(s)	
Level of religious influence	
Political influence	
Decisions made on individualism or collectivism	
Acceptance of hierarchy gap	
Importance of masculinity vs. femininity	
Respect for age	
Personal space and contact	
Direct or indirect communication	
Tolerance of risk	
Handling of time very succinctly or more casual approach to time	
How important are personal relationships to establishing business relationships	
Does "yes" always mean "yes"? Or is it sometimes avoidance of directly saying "no".	
Importance of "Face"	

Business Cards

Item	Answer
Is translation needed?	
Is title important?	
Is there a giving and receiving protocol?	
Other?	

International Launch Plan Step #8

Proper Protocol or Custom for Business Meetings

Action	Proper Protocol or Custom
Initial meeting	
Dress requirement for men	
Dress requirement for women	
Small talk	
Business cards	
Time consideration	
Level of attendees	
Follow up	

Proper Protocol or Custom for Social Entertaining

Action	Proper Protocol or Custom
Social entertaining	
Invitation expectation	
Gifts	
Small talk	
Reciprocation	

International Launch Plan Step #8

Taboos and Deal Breakers

Taboo or Deal Breaker	Why
Religious?	
Food?	
Hand gestures?	
Body language?	
Male/female interaction?	
Level of hierarchy?	

Negotiations

How do the people handle business negotiations?	Answer	How to Counter
Are they aggressive or laid back until the end?		
Are they patient or want a quick resolution?		
Do they employ a loud voice and over-exaggerated body behaviors?		
Do they employ deceitful tactics?		
Do they bargain hard? Is it a game? If so, leave them room in your pricing to bargain.		
Do they partner or go solo?		
Are they direct or indirect?		
Do they offer concessions quickly or wait until the end when you are tired?		
Other?		

Appendix A: INCOTERMS®

Note: Each INCOTERM® must include location of transfer, departure or arrival.

Group	Required Delivery Point	Acronyms	Transfer location
E Departure	The seller makes the goods available at the named place	EXW - Ex Works	Named place of delivery
F Main Carriage Unpaid	The seller/exporter is only responsible to deliver the goods to a carrier named by the buyer	FAS - Free Alongside Ship	Named port of shipment
		FCA - Free Carrier	Named place of delivery
		FOB - Free on Board	Named port of shipment
C Main Carriage Paid	The seller contracts and pays for carriage, but it not responsible for costs or risks once the goods have been shipped	CFR - Cost and Freight	Named port of destination
		CIF - Cost, Insurance & Freight	Named port of destination
		CIP - Carriage & Insurance Paid to	Named place of destination
		CPT - Carriage Paid to	Named place of destination
D Arrival	The seller is responsible for all costs associated with bringing goods to the "named place or port"	DAP - Delivered at Place	Named place of destination
		DAT - Delivered at Terminal	Named terminal at port of place of destination
		DDP - Delivered Duty Paid	Named place of destination

Appendix B: Government Agencies and Other Regulations

International
- ✪ GATT-General Treaty on Trade & Tariff
- ICC-International Chamber of Commerce
- IFC-International Finance Corporation
- IMF-International Monetary Fund
- ITC-International Trade Center
- ✪ UCP - 600 Uniform Customs and Practices for Letters of Credit
- UN-United Nations
- World Bank
- WTO-World Trade Organization

United States
- BIS-Bureau of Industry & Security
- DOC-Department of Commerce
- Department of State
- Department of Treasury
- SBA (Small Business Administration)
- ExIm Bank
- FAS-Foreign Agricultural Services
- OPIC-Overseas Private Investment Corporation
- USTR-U.S. Trade Representative
- USTDA-U.S. Trade and Development Agency

International Launch Plan Appendices

Contact Information for Government Agencies Involved in the Export Process and Locations in the CFR (Code of Federal Regulations)

1. **Defense Services and Defense Articles**
   * Department of State
   Directorate of Defense Trade Controls
   Tel. (202) 663-2700
   http://www.pmddtc.state.gov/
   http://export.gov/regulation/eg_main_018216.asp
   22 CFR parts 120 through 130

2. **Drugs, Chemicals and Precursors**
   Chemicals: Drug Enforcement Administration
   Office of Diversion Control
   Import-Export Unit
   Tel. (202) 307-4916
   www.deadiversion.usdoj.gov
   21 CFR parts 1311 through 1313

   Controlled Substances: Drug Enforcement Administration
   Office of Diversion Control
   Import-Export Unit
   Tel. (202) 307-7182 or (202) 307-7181
   www.deadiversion.usdoj.gov
   21 CFR 1311 through 1313

   Drugs and Biologics: Food and Drug Administration
   Import/Export
   Tel. (301) 594-3150
   21 U.S.C 301 et seq

   Investigational drugs permitted: Food and Drug Administration
   International Affairs
   Tel. (301) 443-4480
   http://www.fda.gov
   21 CFR 312.1106
   General Information Supplement No. 3 to Part 730 – page 2

3. **Fish and Wildlife Controls, Endangered Species**
   Department of the Interior
   Chief Office of Management Authority
   Tel. (703) 358-2093
   http://www.fws.gov/
   50 CFR 17.21, 17.22, 17.31, 17.32

4. **Foreign Assets and Transactions Controls**
   * Department of Treasury
   Office of Foreign Assets Control, Licensing
   Tel. (202) 622-2480
   http://www.treasury.gov
   31 CFR parts 500 through 590

2012 © Taranis, LLC

International Launch Plan Appendices

5. **Medical Devices**
   Food and Drug Administration
   Office of Compliance
   Tel. (301) 594-4699
   http://www.fda.gov/MedicalDevices/DeviceRegulationandGuidance/Importingand
      ExportingDevices/default.htm
   21 U.S.C. 301 et seq

6. **Natural Gas and Electric Power**
   Department of Energy
   Office of Fuels Programs
   Tel. (202) 586-9482
   http://www.fossil.energy.gov/programs/gasregulation/authorizations/Questions.html
   http://www.energy.gov
   http://www.fossil.energy.gov
   10 CFR 205.300 through 205.379 and 590

7. **Nuclear Materials and Equipment**
   * Nuclear Regulatory Commission
   Office of International Programs
   Tel. (301) 415-2344
   http://www.nrc.gov/about-nrc/ip/export-import.html
   10 CFR part 110

8. **Nuclear Technology, Technical Data for Nuclear Weapons/Special Nuclear Materials**
   * Department of Energy
   Office of Export Control Policy & Cooperation (NA-24)
   Tel. (202) 586- 2331
   http://www.energy.gov
   10 CFR part 810

9. **Ocean Freight Forwarders**
   Federal Maritime Commission
   http://www.fmc.gov/
   General Information Supplement No. 3 to Part 730

10. **Miscellaneous**
    Food Safety and Inspection Services
    http://www.fsis.usda.gov/Regulations_%26_Policies/International_Affairs/index.asp

    Animal and Plant Export Inspection Service
    http://www.aphis.usda.gov/import_export/plants/plant_exports/index.shtml

    Electric current abroad
    http://www.ita.doc.gov/media/publications/pdf/current2002final.pdf

Appendix C: Sample Documents

Sales Representation and Distributorship Contract

June 3, 2011

Earnie Earl's Sporting Goods
#4566 Hwy. 175
Gun Barrel, TX 79077

SALES REPRESENTATION and DISTRIBUTORSHIP CONTRACT

Con and Fiona Finn: Outback Gift Shop,

This letter, when signed by you and returned to us, shall constitute the Agreement between us governing your appointment as our Exclusive Sales Representative and Distributor in Australia.

We appoint you our Exclusive Sales Representative and Distributor for the sale within the Territory of those products covered by this Agreement, subject to the terms and conditions set forth in this letter. By your signature you accept the appointment and agree to all of the terms hereof.

1. The "Products" covered by this Agreement are all those products appearing in the catalog that is enclosed herewith and such catalogs as we shall send you in the future and identify as being subject to the Agreement.

2. "Promotion of Sales". You agree to call regularly on all prospective purchasers in the Territory, and to plan an effective sales program. You also agree that during the term of this Agreement you will not act for any principal whose products, noted above in catalog compete with those of Earnie Earl's Sporting Goods unless previously agreed upon in writing.

3. "Authority to Purchase". You are authorized to purchase merchandise covered by this Agreement for your account at prices and terms as set forth in our most recent price list, a copy of which is attached. All orders for Products purchased by you are subject to acceptance or rejection by us.

4. "Purchase of Products". You will neither be entitled to, nor will you be paid any commission on sales we make to you as our distributor pursuant to the terms of Paragraph #3, above.

5. "Authority to Sell". You are further authorized to solicit orders from commercial buyers (other than other than yourself) in your territory for Products covered by this Agreement at prices and terms which are in effect at that time. All orders are subject to acceptance or rejection by us.

6. "Commissions". Will be paid on orders solicited by you according to the terms of Paragraph #5, above for Products shipped by us during the term of this Agreement to purchasers in your territory and accepted and paid for by the purchaser. The commissions for such sales will be established as per the attached schedule which may be adjusted from time to time. Commissions will be paid by the last day of the month, in the month of completion of each shipment.

7. "Terms and Conditions of Sale". All sales to you shall be subject to the terms and conditions set forth on the price lists sent to you from time to time.

8. "Major Tenders". It is agreed that we will advise you of all major tenders received by us to give you the opportunity to quote. Should you be either unwilling or unable to quote any specific tender, we then shall be free to quote directly without any compensation for you.

9. "Use of Catalogs and Advertising Materials". It is understood that you will not use out catalogs or other advertising materials without our written consent.

10. "Expenses" It is understood that we shall not be responsible for any expenses which you may incur in the performance of this contract. It is also understood that you will not be responsible for any expenditures incurred by us.

11. "Trademarks". You bind yourself not to register, use, or permit the use in your name of any trademarks, trade dress, brands, labels, labeling, designs or other indicia of ownership resembling those which are used on goods sold by us, or any other of our suppliers, nor to associate the name directly or indirectly to any business with which you are associated. These obligations shall survive the termination or expiration of this Agreement.

12. "Independent Contractor". You shall be an independent contractor and shall not enter into or assume any obligations on our behalf, nor shall you make any obligations on our behalf, nor shall you make any guarantees, warrantees or representation of the Products on our behalf.

13. "Terms of the Agreement". This agreement, when signed by you and returned to us, shall become effective as of the date of this letter and shall be valid for a period of one year, effective this date, and shall be automatically renewed for similar periods of one year unless either party, prior to 90 days of expiration, serves written notice to the other informing him of his desire not to renew the contract. If this Agreement is so terminated by either party, the other party shall not be entitled to damages or compensation of any nature, regardless of any expenditures or loss of future profit incurred by such other party. Also, in such cases you agree to return to us all samples, catalogs, price lists and other materials belonging to us, within 30 days.

14. "Applicable Law". The rights and duties of the parties to this agreement shall be governed by the laws of the State of Texas, USA.

15. "Arbitration and/or Mediation". Any disagreements are to be settled with Arbitration and/or Mediation governed by the laws of the State of Texas, USA.

Signed:

_____   _____
Earnie Earl & Bettie Sue Taylor   Date:
Earnie Earl's Sporting Goods
Gun Barrel City, TX

Accepted by:

_____   _____
                                        Date:
Con & Fiona Finn
Outback Gift Shop
Darwin, Australia

Source: Hal Jacobson

International LAUNCH Plan Appendices

Pro Forma Invoice

PRO FORMA INVOICE
EARNIE EARL'S SPORTING GOODS
#4566 HWY. 175
GUN BARREL, TX 79077
PH 903-456-7789 903-456-7790 FX

PREPARED FOR:
OUTBACK GIFT SHOP
Hwy. 333, No. 3366
Darwin, NSW 1000 Australia
61-2-9364-9877
61-2-9364-9899 FX

Date: April 07, 2011
Reference: Apr 6, 2011 FX
Suspense Date: June 06, 2011
Shipment: 60 days after receipt
           acceptable L/C
Terms: At site, Irrevocable
       Letter of Credit/USA bank

QUANTITY	DESCRIPTION	PRICE	EXTENSION
1000	License Plates Decorative Outback Tough	$10.00 USD	$10,000.00
	Frt to Houston Port		$300.00
	Ocean Frt to Port of Sydney, Australia		$700.00
	Insurance		$200.00
	CIF, Gun Barrel, TX to Port of Sydney Australia		$11,200.00

Suggested Insurance Coverage-" All Risk-Door to Door"
Title of the goods shall change hands at the port of import, Sydney, Australia
All import fees, isnpection fees and inland transport is the respnsibility of the buyer
Ocean freight & Insurance subject to confirmation.
See attached instructions for opening Letters of Credit.

HTS# 83.10.00.0000
ECCN: EAR-99
Weights & Measure
Gross Lbs   1,000
Gross Kilos 454kgs
Measure- 5-crates 3' x 3' x 2' or 18c.f/total 90cf =2.55cm

" THESE COMMODITIES, TECHNOLOGY OR SOFTWARE WERE EXPORTED FROM THE UNITED STATES IN ACCORDANCE WITH THE EXPORT ADMINISTRATION REGULATIONS. DIVERSION CONTRARY TO U.S. LAW PROHIBITED."

International Launch Plan Appendices

Commercial Invoice

COMMERCIAL INVOICE
EARNIE EARL'S SPORTING GOODS
#4566 HWY. 175
GUN BARREL, TX 79077
PH 903-456-7789 903-456-7790 FX

PREPARED FOR:
OUTBACK GIFT SHOP
Hwy. 333, No. 3366
Darwin, NSW 1000 Australia
61-2-9364-9877
61-2-9364-9899 FX

Date: April 07, 2011
Invoice: # 456678
P.O.# 08061983
Suspense Date: NA
Shipment: 60 days after receipt acceptable L/C
Terms: At site, Irrevocable Letter of Credit/USA bank

QUANTITY	DESCRIPTION	PRICE	EXTENSION
1000	License Plates Decorative Outback Tough	$10.00 USD	$10,000.00

Frt to Houston Port	$300.00
Ocean Frt to Port of Sydney, Australia	$700.00
Insurance	$200.00
CIF, Gun Barrel, TX to Port of Sydney Australia	$11,200.00

Suggested Insurance Coverage-" All Risk-Door to Door"
Title of the goods shall change hands at the port of import, Sydney, Australia
All import fees, isnpection fees and inland transport is the respnsibility of the buyer
Ocean freight & Insurance subject to confirmation.
See attached instructions for opening Letters of Credit.

HTS# 83.10.00.0000
ECCN: EAR-99
Weights & Measure
Gross Lbs   1,000
Gross Kilos 454kgs
Measure- 5-crates 3' x 3' x 2' or 18c.f/total 90cf =2.55cm

" THESE COMMODITIES, TECHNOLOGY OR SOFTWARE WERE EXPORTED FROM THE UNITED STATES IN ACCORDANCE WITH THE EXPORT ADMINISTRATION REGULATIONS. DIVERSION CONTRARY TO U.S. LAW PROHIBITED."

International Launch Plan Appendices

Bill of Lading

Date July 15, 2011   BILL OF LADING – SHORT FORM – NOT NEGOTIABLE   Page 1 of 1

SHIP FROM	Bill of Lading Number: 06231414428569855
Earnie Earl"s Sporting Goods #4566 HWY. 175 Gun Barrel City, TX 79077 SID No.:	BAR CODE SPACE
SHIP TO	Carrier Name: BLUE MOON EXPRESS As agents for Exact Shipping Transportation, Inc.
Outback Gift Shop, HWY 333, NO. 3366, Darwin, NSW, 1000 Australia Delivery to: Port of Sydney Delivery transfer: MIST Terminal/Exact Shipping Transportation, Inc. CID No.:	Trailer number: 336781 Serial number(s): OE336889
THIRD PARTY FREIGHT CHARGES BILL TO	SCAC: BMEX
[Name] [Street Address] [City, ST ZIP Code]	Pro Number: EEAU7 BAR CODE SPACE
Special Instructions: Consign to Order of Shipper. NOTIFY	Freight Charge Terms (Freight charges are prepaid unless marked otherwise): Prepaid ___ ☐ Collect ☐ 3rd Party ☐ _ Master bill of lading with attached underlying bills of lading.

CUSTOMER ORDER INFORMATION

Customer Order No.	# of Packages	Weight	Pallet/Slip (circle one)		Additional Shipper Information
License Plate, Custom Order as per INV#08061983	5 crates	454kg	Y	N	#1 of 5 Port of Sydney, Australia
			Y	N	
	C Ft.	90	Y	N	
	C,M.	2.55	Y	N	
Grand Total					

CARRIER INFORMATION

Handling Unit		Package		Weight	HM (X)	Commodity Description Commodities requiring special or additional care or attention in handling or stowing must be so marked and packaged as to ensure safe transportation with ordinary care. See Section 2(e) of NMFC item 360	LTL Only	
Qty	Type	Qty	Type				NMFC No.	Class
5	plts	5	crates	454 kg		License Plates, Decorative, Base Metal 6" x '12" x 1/16"	1545-03	70
						5 crates, 200 per crate, total 1000 pcs		
						Container #33567899 on board Blue Moon Express		
						Freight prepaid see INV. #08061983		
						HTS 83.10.00.0000		
						ECCN-EAR-99		

" THESE COMMODITIES, TECHNOLOGY OR SOFTWARE WERE EXPORTED FROM THE UNITED STATES IN ACCORDANCE WITH THE EXPORT ADMINISTRATION REGULATIONS. DIVERSION CONTRARY TO U.S. LAW PROHIBITED."

Where the rate is dependent on value, shippers are required to state specifically in writing the agreed or declared value of the property as follows: "The agreed or declared value of the property is specifically stated by the shipper to be not exceeding _____ per _____."

Amount: $ 11,200 CIF/ $10,300 FOB Houston, TX/ _____
Fee terms: Collect Prepaid XXX

Note: Liability limitation for loss or damage in this shipment may be applicable. See 49 USC § 14706(c)(1)(A) and (B).

Received, subject to individually determined rates or contracts that have been agreed upon in writing between the carrier and shipper, if applicable, otherwise to the rates, classifications, and rules that have been established by the carrier and are available to the shipper, on request, and to all applicable state and federal regulations.	The carrier shall not make delivery of this shipment without payment of charges and all other lawful fees. Shipper Signature _____		
Shipper Signature/Date	Trailer Loaded: ¯ By shipper _ By driver	Freight Counted: ¯ By shipper _ By driver/pallets said to contain _ By driver/pieces	Carrier Signature/Pickup Date
This is to certify that the above named materials are properly classified, packaged, marked, and labeled, and are in proper condition for transportation according to the applicable regulations of the DOT.			Carrier acknowledges receipt of packages and required placards. Carrier certifies emergency response information was made available and/or carrier has the DOT emergency response guidebook or equivalent documentation in the vehicle. Property described above is received in good order, except as noted.

International Launch Plan Appendices

Certificate of Origin

CERTIFICATE OF ORIGIN
FOR GENERAL USE

The undersigned <u>Jimmy John, Notary, Mabank, TX, Chamber of Commerce</u>
(Owner or Agent, or Co)

for <u>Earnie Earl's Sporting Goods</u> declares
(Name and Address of Shipper)

that the following mentioned goods shipped on <u>July 15, 2011</u>
(Name of Ship)
on the date <u>July 15, 2011</u> consigned to <u>Order of Shipper</u> are the product of the United States of America.

MARKS AND NUMBERS	NO. OF PKGS BOXES OR CASES	WEIGHT IN KILOS		DESCRIPTION
		GROSS	NET	
5 Crates/ Mark #1 to #5	5	454	420	License Plates, Base Metal, Decorative, 6" x 12" x 1/16" Schedule B# - 83.10.00

STATE OF Texas
COUNTY OF Kaufman

Sworn to before me
This <u>13</u> day of <u>July</u> <u>2011</u>   *Jimmy John*
                                                            (Signature of Owner or Agent)

The <u>Mabank, TX, Chamber of Commerce, 1567 Hwy 175, Mabank, TX , 79078, USA</u>
A recognized Chamber of Commerce under the laws of the state of <u>TX</u>, has examined the
the manufacturer's invoice or shipper's affidavit concerning the origin of the merchandise and, according to the best
of its knowledge and belief, finds that the products named originated in the United States of North America.

FORM X101 REV. 7-92   Secretary *Billy Bob*

Certificate of Insurance

Ocean Cargo - Certificate of Insurance

This certifies that the Assured is insured under and subject to the conditions of the policy in this Certificate. **Assured:** Earnie Earl's Sporting Goods Store **Loss payable to:** Earnie Earl & Betty Sue Taylor	Policy #468895	Certificate # 76A32
	Issued Date: 7-13-11	Ship Date: 7-15-11
	Place of Issue: Gun Barrel City, TX	

Conveyance: Blue Moon Express	Insured Value USD: $12,320.00
Additional Carrier Information: Exact Shipping Transportation Inc.	

Place of Origin: Gun Barrel, TX	Final Destination: Sydney, Australia
Country of Origin: USA	Destination Country: Australia
Port of Loading: Houston, TX	Port of Discharge: Sydney Australia
Country of Loading: USA	Country of Discharge: Australia

Description of Goods: License Plates-Decorative, Base Metal, 6" x 12" x 1/16" Schedule B #83.10.00

Marks & Numbers: 5 crates, 200 per crate, 1000 pcs total, marked crate 1-5

                Container #33567899 on board Blue Moon Express

Pieces & Weights: 1000 pcs, 454kg / 90 cubic feet / 2.55cm

Average Terms & Conditions: Insured property while shipped on deck of an ocean vessel subject to an ON DECK bill of lading is warranted Free from Particular Average unless caused by the vessel being stranded, sunk or burnt but not withstanding this Warranty, the Company is to pay any physical loss of or damage to the insured property which may be reasonable attributed to fire, collision or contact of the vessel with any external substance other than water, or to discharge of cargo at port of distress but including jettison and or washing overboard.
This insurance covers against "All Risks" of physical loss or damage from any external cause but excluding: war, strikes, riots, seizure, detention.

CONDITIONS: This insurance, in addition to the foregoing, is subject to the following American Institute Cargo Clauses inclusive of but not limited to: (see explanations and extended list)
    Basic Exclusion   General Averaging   Economic & Trade Sanctions
    Both to Blame   Refused/Returned   Consolidation/Deconsolidation

PARAMOUNT WARRANTIES: F.C. & S Warranty   S.R. & C. C. Warranty   Delay Warranty

SUBROGATION AND IMPAIRMENT OF RECOVERY: It is a condition of this insurance that upon payment of any loss, the Company shall be subrogated to all rights and claims against third parties arising out of such loss.

SUIT: No suit or action for the recovery of any claim arising under this Certification shall be maintainable in any Court unless such suit shall have been commenced within two years of the happening of the loss.

Signed: *Earnie Earl & Betty Sue Taylor*	Date: July 13, 2011

International LAUNCH Plan Appendices

Key for 700 Format Specifications (Letter of Credit)

MT 700 Issue of a Documentary Credit

Status	Tag	Field Name	Content/Options	No.
M	27	Sequence of Total	1!n/1!n	1
M	40A	Form of Documentary Credit	24x	2
M	20	Documentary Credit Number	16x	3
O	23	Reference to Pre-Advice	16x	4
O	31C	Date of Issue	6!n	5
M	31D	Date and Place of Expiry	6!n29x	6
O	51a	Applicant Bank	A or D	7
M	50	Applicant	4*35x	8
M	59	Beneficiary	[/34x] 4*35x	9
M	32B	Currency Code, Amount	3!a15d	10
O	39A	Percentage Credit Amount Tolerance	2n/2n	11
O	39B	Maximum Credit Amount	13x	12
O	39C	Additional Amounts Covered	4*35x	13
M	41a	Available With ... By ...	A or D	14
O	42C	Drafts at ...	3*35x	15
O	42a	Drawee	A or D	16

Status	Tag	Field Name	Content/Options	No.
O	42M	Mixed Payment Details	4*35x	17
O	42P	Deferred Payment Details	4*35x	18
O	43P	Partial Shipments	1*35x	19
O	43T	Transhipment	1*35x	20
O	44A	Loading on Board/Dispatch/Taking in Charge at/from ...	1*65x	21
O	44B	For Transportation to ...	1*65x	22
O	44C	Latest Date of Shipment	6!n	23
O	44D	Shipment Period	6*65x	24
O	45A	Description of Goods and/or Services	100*65x	25
O	46A	Documents Required	100*65x	26
O	47A	Additional Conditions	100*65x	27
O	71B	Charges	6*35x	28
O	48	Period for Presentation	4*35x	29
M	49	Confirmation Instructions	7!x	30
O	53a	Reimbursing Bank	A or D	31
O	78	Instructions to the Paying/Accepting/Negotiating Bank	12*65x	32
O	57a	'Advise Through' Bank	A, B or D	33
O	72	Sender to Receiver Information	6*35x	34

M = Mandatory O = Optional

Sample Letter of Credit Received Through SWIFT

FIN 700 Issue
27: sequence of total
1/1
40A: form of documentary credit
IRREVOCABLE
20: documentary credit no.
LIC 12345
31C: date of issue
2011/06/30
31D: date and place of expiry
2011/08/20
50: applicant
OUTBACK GIFT SHOP
DARWIN, AUSTRALIA
59: beneficiary
EARNIE EARL'S SPORTING GOODS
GUN BARREL CITY, TX
32B: currency code amount
Currency: USD
Amount: 11,200.00
39A: percentage credit amount tolerance
none
41A: available with/by
ANY BANK BY NEGOTIATION
42C: drafts at
SIGHT
42A: drawee
ISSUING BANK
43P: partial shipments
NOT ALLOWED
43T: transshipment
NOT ALLOWED
44A: on board/disp/taking charge
PORT OF HOUSTON,TX
44B: for transportation to
SYDNEY, AUSTRALIA
44C: latest date of shipment
2011/07/15
45A: descr goods and/or services
+ 1,000 EA. DECORATIVE BASE METAL LICENSE PLATES @USD $10 EA PER PURCHASE ORDER NO. 08061983 CIF SYDNEY
46A: documents required
+COMMERCIAL INVOICE CERTIFYING THAT THE MERCHANDISE CONFORMS TO PURCHASE ORDER SPECIFICATIONS +FULL SET OF OCEAN BILLS OF LADING CONSIGNED TO THE ORDER OF BANK OF AUSTRALIA MARKED NOTIFY BLUEMOON INTERNATIONAL MARKED FREIGHT PREPAID
48: period for presentation
WITHIN 21 DAYS AFTER SHIPMENT
49: confirmation instructions
WITHOUT
78: instructions to pay/acc/neg bk
+REIMBURSEMENT WILL BE PROVIDED TO NEGOTIATING BANK UPON RECEIPT OF THE DOCUMENTS AT OUR COUNTERS.

International Launch Plan Appendices

Export Compliance Manual

Earnie Earl's Sporting Goods Export Compliance Manual							
1. Management Commitment (signed pledge + companywide letter of Export Compliance Program)							
We, Ernie Earl & Betty Sue, do solemnly swear to do our duty to uphold every letter, number							
semicolon and comma of the CFR-15 to the best of our ability.							
Signed:	Ernie Earl & Betty Sue						
2. Risk Analysis							
Item	Country	Code	Date of Order	Invoice			
License Plate	AU	LP1-AU	3/4/2011	245			
Purse	CL	P1-CL	4/6/2011	345			
Sauce	HK	S1-HK	6/9/2011	567			
Goggles-Night	ZA	GNV1-ZA	8/7/2011	877			
Cream-Sun	IE	CS1-IE	9/2/2011	879			
Item Code	Low	Medium	High	Reason	Lic	Other	
LP1-AU	x				no		
P1-CL	x				no		
S1-HK	x				no		
GNV1-ZA		x		BIS	yes		
CS1-IE	x					health cert	
3. Export Compliance Manual Policy							
Action Required & Information Gathered on **EACH** Initial Transaction w/ Audits							
Item	4?	Port Exp	Port Imp	Schedule B	ECCN	ITN	#7 Audit
LP1-AU							
P1-CH							
S1-HK							
GNV1-SA							
4. Training							
Name	Position	Type	Date Completed				
Betty Sue	COO	Export	Nov. 3, 2011				
5. Cradle to Grave Export Compliance Security							
see #2 & #3							
6. Recordkeeping							
min. 5yrs.							
7. Export Compliance Monitoring & Audit							
see #3							
8. Problems							
None to date							
9. Corrective Action							
None to date							

9 Key Components for the Export Compliance Manual
1. Management Commitment
2. Risk Analysis
3. Export Compliance Manual Policy
4. Training
5. Export Compliance Security
6. Recordkeeping
7. Monitoring & Audits
8. Problems
9. Corrective Action

2012 © Taranis, LLC